The Book of
DANGEROUS
COCKTAILS

The Book of

DANGEROUS COCKTAILS

Adventurous Recipes for Serious Drinkers

CASTLE POINT BOOKS
NEW YORK

DYLAN MARCH and JENNIFER BOUDINOT

Printed in the United States of America.
For information, address St. Martin's Press,
175 Fifth Avenue, New York, N.Y. 10010.

www.castlepointbooks.com
www.stmartins.com

The Castle Point Books trademark is owned by Castle Point Publishing, LLC.
Castle Point books are published and distributed by St. Martin's Press, LLC.

Cover design by Robert Grom
Interior design by SMAY Design/Phil Yarnall

The Library of Congress Cataloging-in-Publication Data is available upon request.

ISBN 978-1-250-10884-5

Our books may be purchased in bulk for promotional, educational, or business use.
Please contact your local bookseller or the Macmillan Corporate and
Premium Sales Department at 1-800-221-7945, extension 5442,
or by e-mail at MacmillanSpecialMarkets@macmillan.com.

First Edition: October 2016

2 4 6 8 10 9 7 5 3 1

WARNING:

The drinks in this book are potentially dangerous if used without appropriate precautions. Please use caution when consuming alcoholic beverages, especially alcoholic beverages that contain marijuana. The mixture of alcohol and marijuana may affect you in unexpected ways. Please only consume these drinks in the safety of your own home. When making drinks that include fire or infusing liquor, keep all combustible materials safely away from your workspace. Do not use any flame, including from a gas stove, when infusing liquor. Always keep a fire extinguisher handy. Being dangerous doesn't mean ignoring safety!

ACKNOWLEDGMENTS

Thanks to Jen Boudinot and the whole Castle Point team for bringing this project to me and trusting me with it. Thanks to Phil Yarnall for a great design and to photographer Herminio Torres for bringing my drinks to visual life (and being a great friend). Thank you to Belle Shoals, Botanic Lab, and La Loba Cantina for allowing us to shoot at their beautiful bars.

To all the bar teams I have worked with: you are, and continue to be, my professors in nerdy cocktail education. Special thanks to my tattoo buddy Lindsey Moore and to Josh Mazza—you are a great mentor and your joy and unending drive for excellence inspire me. To Jonny and Christy Sheehan and the rest of the Bar Chord family, thanks for giving me my start and nurturing my constant experimentation.

Thank you to all of my colleagues and friends who contributed drinks and more to this project, including Rob Giles, Caleb Mayes, Phil Barlow, Hannah Caner, Eric Moore, Etan Grun, Nati Rabinowitz (Northpoint Negroni), Tad Carducci (The Crippler), Audrey Saunders (Gin-Gin Mule), Francis Verrall (Captain Redbeard's Punch, Watermelon Limeade, Abigal Sponder, Old Oscar, Breakfast in Brooklyn), Jack Crown (Absinthe Daiquiri), Josh Mazza (Sleepy Hollow), and JJ Condon (Banks' Cadaver, Valentine's Kiss, Remember Scotland).

Finally, to my family—Mom, Dad, Brad, and Tyler—I love you more than everything. Thank you for your unending love and support.

—*Dylan March*

Contents

THE BOOK OF DANGEROUS COCKTAILS: ADVENTUROUS RECIPES FOR SERIOUS DRINKERS

Introduction

Before you jump into the
dangerously delicious,
dangerously boozy, and
dangerously drug-infused
cocktails in this book, find out
what you need to know about
stocking your bar, making drinks,
and infusing liquor with weed.

Inside this book you'll find the craziest, most baller, cancel-your-plans-because-you-were-drunk-two-hours-ago cocktails that might just burn off your tongue. Just kidding: this is a serious cocktail book. And while the drinks inside will definitely get you fucked up, and some of them involve fire, they're not massive bathtub punches full of Everclear with the express purpose of giving you a massive hangover (well, OK, one of them is—see page 91).

That's right, we're not messing around. We're serious cocktail people, and Dylan even has professional cred, having worked as a craft bartender in NYC for eight years. Jen, a cookbook author, used to be a regular at one of his bars, and after many late nights watching him shoot absinthe out of his mouth while lighting it on fire (please don't try that at home (or anywhere), folks) *The Book of Dangerous Cocktails* was born.

What is a dangerous cocktail? It's simply a drink that's delicious, a tad mysterious, and either dangerously easy to drink or dangerous to drink too many of. Along with original cocktail recipes and classics with a twist, we've included party punches, flamers (drinks you can light on fire), and boozy shooters. And in the last chapter, we'll give you drinks you can make with the most badass weapon in your cocktail arsenal: weed-infused liquor.

So strap yourself in and get ready for a ride—not so much a rollercoaster, but an informative, boozy riverboat tour with two snarky yet enthusiastic guides who met at a bar. Before we get to the cocktails, though, we have some basic knowledge to drop about the kinds of booze and mixers you should be buying to make the cocktails, how to properly construct them, and how to infuse weed into any bottle of liquor on hand.

STOCKING YOUR BAR

When making cocktails, nothing is more important than having the right ingredients. Anyone who bought a giant plastic bottle of vodka to get them through the weekends at college knows how shitty cheap booze can be. So spring for the good stuff. When you're at the liquor store, you don't necessarily have to buy the most expensive bottle on the shelf, but do spend the extra money to buy a spirit that is made from quality ingredients, aged

an appropriate amount of time, and given personal attention from someone who cares about the way it tastes. Small-batch liquors from local distilleries not only taste better, their variances in flavor due to regional ingredients and tastes can lead you to discover something about a spirit you never realized. In other words, spending a little more on high-quality booze actually makes you a better drinker! And if being a more-refined human being isn't enough to rationalize buying high-quality booze, you should also know that a good collection

of liquors, liqueurs, and yes, some bitters is even sexier than a good collection of vintage porn.

How much liquor you decide to keep on hand is up to you. Dylan keeps a rather modest home bar, with a relatively small collection of curated spirits, including one or two good bottles of gin, rye, bourbon, and scotch, as well as a variety of liqueurs and other modifiers to play around with. When he finishes a bottle of something, he replaces it with something else he'd like to try. Meanwhile, Jen always has a couple days' supply of weed and probably just enough booze to make sure that if she brings a guy home, he doesn't have a reason to leave before the night is through. But even though she's not the type of person to keep vermouth, fernet, and elderflower liqueur around the house, she does like to pick a cocktail or two to make when having parties, and there's no better gift for special occasions than infusing a bottle of mezcal with weed.

Following is a comprehensive list of all the liquors, modifiers, and more we use in this book. By no means do we expect you to buy them all! But use this list as a quick reference for our preferred brands and as a cipher for some of our more exotic ingredients (what? you don't know what Ouzo is?). Or, you know, read it if you're just one of those people who likes to know stuff.

Vodka

Ah, vodka. For many of us, it ushered us into this fantastical world called drunkenness, with practically no aftertaste and with almost as many available flavors as a Kool-Aid. But vodka can be for grown-ups, too—just ask anyone from the Eastern

Bloc. And while you're at it, ask them to get you a locally made bottle of potato vodka the next time they're home. They're so tasty, with distinct vegetal notes, that you'll want to sip them like whiskey. If you don't have an overseas connection, we recommend Boyd & Blair, which makes their vodka with small batches of potatoes. For corn vodka, which has a sweeter finish and is much easier to find in the US, we recommend Spring44. Some high-end vodkas like Grey Goose (Jen's favorite for Martinis) are even made of wheat!

By the way, there is such thing as "high proof" vodka, but as it mostly tastes like diesel fuel we've left it out of this book, and stuck with classier vodka-based drinks like Dylan's original the Moving Fjord (page 38) and fun classics like the Sex on the Beach (page 37).

Gin

If you're like Jen, you didn't have much of a taste for gin until one night when you tried it again, and then wanted to drink nothing else ever again. Gin is made primarily from juniper berries, but also contains a variety of botanicals like coriander, sage, orange peel, cucumber, and rosemary. A distillery tweaking the amounts and kinds of botanicals based on their personal tastes and what's locally available can have a major impact on the taste of gin, so make sure to keep an eye out for small batches for experimentation purposes, especially if you're looking for a good gin to infuse with weed.

Many of the drinks you'll find in this book contain "navy strength" gin. Dating back to the eighteenth century, navy strength gin was drunk

by sailors in the British Royal Navy to fight scurvy. The Brits decreed that it needed to be 114 proof (57 percent alcohol by volume) to be truly effective, and to get everyone truly fucked up.

There are lots of great distilleries that make navy strength gin, but our favorites are New York Distilling Company (which makes Perry's Tot Gin) and Plymouth. Plymouth gin is bit sweeter, and Perry's Tot is more clean and dry. We also love the gins made by Spring44. Their Mountain Gin is perfect for infusing weed, and they also make an Old Tom gin (barrel-aged, malty, sweeter) that is simply delicious.

In chapter two, we've adapted a bunch of gin-based cocktails—some classics, some originals—for navy strength gin to give them an extra dose of booziness. Navy strength gin is considerably dryer and hotter, so if you can't handle it, simply scale them back down to regular strength.

Whiskey

When you think of someone striding into a cow-boy bar and throwing back a bracing drink, you probably think of whiskey. And although the deep, pronounced flavor of single malt Scotches can be a lot for novice drinkers to handle, there are plenty of gentler blends, ryes, and bourbons.

As you may know, bourbon is whiskey made from primarily corn, and it's as American as apple pie. Traditionally (and legally) at least 80 proof, it has a distinctive woody flavor thanks to being aged in charred oak barrels. Our favorite bourbons are Bulleit and Elijah Craig Small Batch. New corn whiskey (also known as white corn whiskey, moonshine, or white dog) is a clear or almost-clear spirit that hasn't been aged or aged only a couple of years. A bit of a fad, there are still some super-interesting small batch corn whiskeys (like Mellow Corn), and you'll find a couple of drinks containing them on pages 88–89.

Like bourbon, rye whiskey is also an American invention. Dryer than most bourbons, ryes also have a peppery taste and tend to be more layered and complex. Our favorites are Bulleit, Old Overholt, and High West.

Finally, in this book you'll also find drinks featuring Irish whiskey, a spirit similar to Scotch but with a smoother finish and less earthy taste. Unlike a single-malt Scotch, Irish whiskey is usually blended from several distilleries. It's also great for infusing weed. Our favorite brand is Tullamore Dew, but we also like two blended Scotches that give you a similar taste to an Irish whiskey: Cutty Sark Prohibition and Monkey Shoulder.

A term you'll see frequently with whiskey in this book is "bonded." This essentially means a high-proof whiskey, although at bars and in the liquor store you'll also see terms like "cask strength," "barrel strength," or "barrel proof"—which imply strong whiskeys that are taken straight from the barrel, with no water added. "Bonded" is technically a legal term that comes from the Bottled in Bond Act of 1897, which set up regulations for America's most popular beverage. A bonded whiskey is one that's produced by a single distillery, aged for at least four years, and, most importantly, bottled at 100 proof (50 percent alcohol by volume)—which is 20 proof higher than the standard for most commercially available whiskeys. Even though many distilleries don't advertise their whiskeys as being legally bonded (due to

a general feeling that the law is outdated and obsolete), we use the term in this book as a catch-all for any whiskey of your choice that's 100 proof or higher, although you'll find many whiskeys on the market that are much more dangerous. For bonded whiskeys, we like Evan Williams and Old Grand-Dad (bonded bourbon), and Rittenhouse (bonded rye).

As for that bracing whiskey shot in the cowboy bar—single-malt Scotch, the "black coffee" of the whiskey word, so revered that the English language even bends the rules and deletes the extra e in "whisky" when referring to it…after you've tried some bourbons and ryes, follow your palate. Some people (like Dylan) enjoy big, in-your-face, peaty, smoky scotches like those from the Islay region (Laphroaig, Lagavulin), while others (like Jen) like more mellow Scotches like Highland Park and Macallan. Increasingly, small-batch Scotches are high-proof, so ask at your local liquor store and see what they have available—whatever it is, you probably won't be disappointed. (And don't forget to explore the single malts out of Japan—they are doing really great things these days!)

Tequila and Mezcal

Tequila and mezcal are Mexican spirits made from the agave plant. While tequila is technically a type of mezcal, when you hear the term "mezcal" (both on the street and in this book), it refers to a spirit that's been growing in popularity in the craft cocktail scene. This mezcal is produced mostly in Oaxaca, rather than near Tequila (yes, Tequila is actually a town in Mexico), and is made from a different kind of agave.

Mezcal differs from tequila in its rich smoky flavor, the attribute that has won it so much love from serious sippers. If you like whiskey, you'll love mezcal. It's

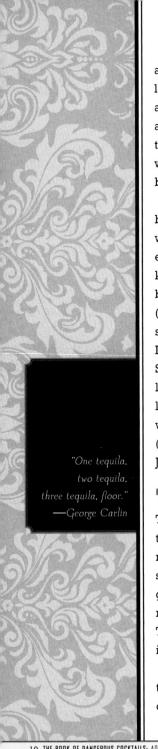

"One tequila,
two tequila,
three tequila, floor."
—George Carlin

also one of the best spirits for infusing with marijuana, thanks both to its flavor and its low pH, which allows for a vivid green color once infused. (See page 20 for more information on how to do this!).

For tequila, we like easy-drinking, agave-forward brands like Olmeca Altos Plata, Casamigos, and Espolòn. For mezcal, we're partial to Ilegal Mezcal, and Dylan also loves Fidencio and Alipús, all of which are on the low end of the smokiness scale. For something a little beefier and oaky, try Mezcal Vago.

Rum

If you go to a party and there are a couple of different types of rum there, you know things could get dangerous. Light or white rum, which (as its name would suggest) is the lightest of rums, is also the youngest. Its clean taste is great for drinks like the Mojito (page 61). We like Denizen, though Bacardi will do fine. Dark rum has been cask-aged a little longer, giving it a richer flavor and color. For dark rum, go with Plantation, which will taste delicious in just about any rum drink in this book. For the darkest rum, black rum, we recommend Gosling's. Finally, there's spiced rum, the most common of which is Captain Morgan. Spiced rum is great for drinks that need some extra spice (naturally) and it's Jen's favorite rum for weed infusions.

This book (or at least, the Dangerously Boozy chapter) wouldn't be complete without overproof rum. Commonly referred to as "151-proof" after Barcardi's offering, overproof rum isn't just one of the cheapest boozes you can buy if you want to light the top of a drink on fire (although it is that, too). Overproof rum that has been made with care, like J Wray & Nephew's, can be complex and fresh *and* knock you on your ass at the same time.

The last thing you need to know about rum is that most rum that's commercially available in the US is molasses-based, but in recent years people have been getting more in to agricole rum (rum made with sugarcane), for good reason. Its freshness and purity elevates any cocktail you'd normally just throw some Bacardi into. It is highly recommended for most of these cocktails.

Absinthe

A high-proof spirit full of mystery, most of what you know about absinthe is probably a myth. It's *not* illegal in the United States (except in places where the sale of high-proof spirits is illegal in general), and it's not true that European versions are therefore completely different that what we get here in America. It's made from a otherwise ordinary shrub called wormwood as well as other botanicals, and has a distinct anise flavor. By and large, absinthe is extremely alcoholic, usually between 60 and 75 proof.

Liqueurs, Amaros, and Other Modifiers

In the bar world, the word "modifier" means a liquid that imparts a particular flavor to a drink that is specific and exclusive to that liquid. These modifiers—ranging from sweet liqueurs to herby apertifs and everything in between—are what turns a mixed drink into a *cocktail*, a beverage that takes art and strategy. There are many wonderful, flavorful ingredients that fall under this category, but here's an as-quick-as-possible rundown of what you'll find in this book:

Vermouth is an essential ingredient in many classic cocktails. Carpano Antica Formula (a.k.a. "Antica") is a sweet vermouth that is considered one of the oldest still in existence. It's hugely popular, thanks to its balanced sweetness and dark and spicy complexity. It's perfect for Manhattans. Punt e Mes, Italian for "point and a half," is a slightly more bitter version of Antica, thought to be a "point" sweet and a "half point" bitter. It is a beautiful, perhaps underused vermouth that works great with a Negroni (page 68) or Red Hook (page 90).

Triple Sec, an orange liqueur, is often known by its most common brand name, Cointreau. It's interchangeable with orange Curaçao, the twin sister of blue Curaçao, which has a similar flavor but an anti-freeze–like color that makes it a classic for tiki drinks like the Blue Hawaiian (page 61).

Cynar, which gets its name from the Latin root for artichoke, is a beautiful, earthy, bitter, complex amaro (infused spirit) made from artichoke as well as a variety of other herbs. It's delicious on its own as a digestif, as well as in cocktails. The higher proof version is called Cynar 70.

Suze, a dry, floral, herbal concoction made from gentian root, is one of Dylan's favorite liqueurs. Similar liqueurs include Saler's, Dimmi, and Aveze.

If an amaro can be controversial, **fernet** is it. Some drink enthusiasts (like Dylan) love it, while others (like Jen) don't get what the big deal is. It has a very distinctive taste, with notes of mint, vanilla, apricot, and licorice. Like Cynar, it is meant as a digestif, but it

can be enjoyed at any time. Fernet-Branca is the most popular brand of fernet, though Letherbee Fernet and Fernet-Vallet by Haas Brothers are fantastic as well.

Campari is a popular Italian liqueur essential to cocktails like the Negroni (page 68). It's bittersweet, with notes of gentian root and citrus. Considered to be a slightly milder form of Campari, **Aperol** is a slightly bitter, bright, and citrusy liqueur that gives off a sweet foretaste with an off-herbal finish.

Known by the brand Kahlúa, **coffee liqueur** is featured in many drinks in this book that end up in mugs. It's counterpart, **Irish cream**, also makes an appearance. If you really like these warm, sometimes dessert-like drinks, try checking out cream liqueurs without "Irish" on the label, like RumChata or Guappa.

Chartreuse has been made by French monks since 1737 and is one of the most prized and appreciated liqueurs around. The production process is held as a high secret among the monks, and while many have attempted to duplicate the flavor, none have come close to succeeding. Green chartreuse is quite herbaceous and high-proof (110), while yellow chartreuse is milder (80 proof) and carries notes of honey. The monastery in France that produces chartreuse also produces various rare forms of their formula that are so prized they're collected as valuable rarities. Chartreuses are a natural pairing for marijuana, and are used in our weed-infused cocktail classics like the Bijou (page 117) and Last Word (page 118).

Lillet Blanc is an aperitif wine that is slightly sweet and essential in many classic cocktails. It's also tasty on its own before dinner. Ask your grandparents about it.

An herbal, sweet, and aromatic French liqueur that's in a category all its own, **Bénédictine** is essential to classics like the Vieux Carré (page 94). **Elderflower liqueur** might be the best secret cocktail ingredients of all time. Now widely available thanks to St. Germain (our favorite brand), it adds a flowery element that complements both sweet and sour flavors. It makes any otherwise-inferior cocktail so drinkable that it's been called "bartenders' ketchup."

Cherry heering is a dark, savory-yet-sweet, layered cherry liqueur that should not be mistaken for or replaced by maraschino liqueur. **Maraschino liqueur** does have its place, however, and is used in many cocktails in this book. Make sure to get a bottle that has a sweet cherry flavor without being overpowering—our favorite brand is Luxardo.

Amaretto is an Italian, almond-flavored liqueur that's used in many of hot drinks in this book. Plus, if you light it on fire with rum and slam it into a class of pilsner, it tastes just like Dr. Pepper! (See page 64).

Other liqueurs of all kinds appear throughout these pages, so make sure to check the index if you have a bottle of something you've been wanting to try in a cocktail. You'll find fruit-based liqueurs like raspberry, pomegranate, strawberry, banana,

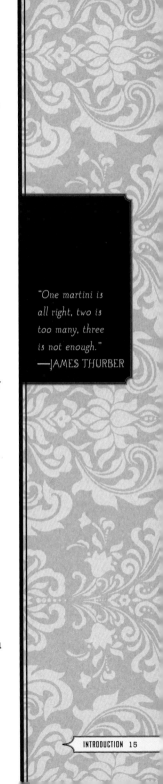

"One martini is all right, two is too many, three is not enough."
—JAMES THURBER

blackberry, and coconut, as well as peach liqueur (Southern Comfort) and crème de cassis—a dark red liqueur made from blackcurrants. Spice-based liqueurs include the minty crème de menthe, Velvet Falernum (a clove-based liqueur from Barbados), and various anise-flavored liqueurs like Sambuca (Italian), Pastis (France), and Ouzo (Greek).

Brandies, which differentiate themselves from liqueurs because they're (usually) not sweetened, are also included throughout. You'll find apricot, orange, and apple-flavored brandy, as well as a recipe using Pisco brandy (page 65), Peru's national spirit. **Schnapps** are similar to brandies (but often of lower quality) and are used here when we absolutely have to—because you couldn't have an authentic Buttery Nipple shooter (page 63) without butterscotch schnapps.

Mixers

Mixers are non-alcoholic ingredients in cocktails, and run the gamut from simple club soda to passion fruit juice (one of the best juices for disguising the taste of booze).

The most important thing to know about mixers is to always use the freshest possible. Make a drink like the Bee's Knees (page 40)—a delicate balance of honey, lemon juice, and gin—with bottled lemon juice, and it tastes like Kombucha gone wrong. With fresh lemon juice, it's not harsh, it's super easy to drink, and it tastes like a sophisticated cocktail even though it only has three ingredients. So invest in an $8 citrus reamer (or just use one of the beaters of an electric mixer, which is basically the same thing) and stop being lazy.

As for the cranberry, apple, and ginger juices (yes, ginger juice, a far-superior alternative to ginger beer), we're cool if you buy those at the store.

You'll find that most of the drinks in this collection also contain **bitters.** Highly concentrated infusions of botanicals, herbs, and spices, bitters are basically like a spice rack specifically for cocktail-making. Bitters have been around for as long as booze has, but they're having a resurgence as people start to learn more about making good drinks. You can find bitters in just about every flavor under the sun—a couple of favorites you'll find here are orange bitters and celery bitters—but many companies have also made their own propriety bitter blends that have worked their way into cocktail doctrine, thanks to their inclusion in early cocktails that we still drink (or drink versions of) today.

Probably the most well-known bitters blend is Angostura aromatic bitters. Named after the city in Venezuela in which they're from, they're made with gentian root and have notes of cinnamon, cardamom, and nutmeg, which go well with a lot of different varieties of booze, kind of like Coca-cola. (The Angostura company now also makes a version of orange bitters.) At around the same time as Angostura bitters were being developed in Venezuela (the 1830s–40s), Peychaud's bitters were being developed in New Orleans. (See page 95 for more on Peychaud and his signature drink, the Sazerac). Both were originally used for medicinal purposes, but they quickly caught on with the recreational set.

Syrups are the sweet counterpart to bitters. Most of the cocktails in this book contain simple syrup, which is a sugar-water mixture you can make at home: Simply heat equal amounts water and sugar in a saucepan until the sugar is dissolved. Some cocktails contain grenadine, a pomegranate syrup you can find at liquor stores, and a few cocktails contain some fancier syrups, like spiced demerara syrup and almond-orgeat. For these, do a Google search or look at a shop that sells fine foods.

Garnishes

Last but not least, we have garnishes. OK, truth be told, they kind of *are* the least important part of a drink—no one is going to turn away your carefully crafted cocktail with a clever name just because it doesn't have that candied wheel of ginger on top. But we've included garnishes throughout that we feel give the drinks they accompany a little extra flavor boost and sometimes a little extra excitement—such as in the case with our flaming orange peel garnishes and the garnish on the Magic Dragon Margarita (page 125), which is illegal in most states. (Unless it's more medicinal purposes, of course.)

Tools of the Trade

Obviously, people make cocktails at home all the time by using a capped thermos as a shaker and eyeing up the measurements. But having a few proper bar tools handy makes your job easier and definitely adds to your cocktail cred. Plus, you can buy a shaker with a strainer for less than five bucks! Start there, then get a real jigger and a twisty bar spoon (like the one Dylan has tattooed on his arm). Add a muddler, a zester, and a bottle opener and you have a complete bar set.

Next up, how's your glass collection? In this book we use a wide variety of glasses, from highballs to rocks to Champagne flutes. While these are listed mostly for professionals, a quick Google search for the name of the listed glass will turn up the specs of what you *should* be putting these drinks into to best extenuate their nose (aroma), keep them cold, and other concerns. Even if you can't afford a Crate & Barrel shopping spree, try ducking into Goodwill and seeing what you can pick up, until you have a whole collection. But if you just want to use the glass in your cabinet that's the closest fit to the amount of liquid you have, that will probably do too.

INFUSING SPIRITS WITH MARIJUANA

The third chapter of this book features cocktails that contain weed-infused liquor. There are a lot of animated gifs that express just how stonerifically fantastic this is, but this is book. So use your imagination (that animated gif generator in your brain) and get excited.

Infusing liquor with weed is relatively simple, as long as you don't burn your house down. No, seriously—being dangerous means living on the edge, but if you go over the edge you lose, in the form of an early death. ***Alcohol, and even alcohol fumes, are extremely flammable. Do NOT infuse liquor over a gas burner or near any other open flame, under any circumstances. Work in a well-ventilated area and do NOT improvise. "Fiery drug death" is not how you want to go down.*** Use a bit of caution is what we're saying.

There are a few different methods for alcohol-weed infusions. The simplest is to simply leave some bud in a bottle of booze for about a year, then pour it through some cheesecloth and chug-a-lug! It won't look too pretty, but stoner legend has it that this is an effective way to draw out the small amount of THC that resides in marijuana stems, so if you don't mind a brownish, cloudy infusion that takes time over effort, this might be the method for you.

The more popular (and way quicker) technique, however, uses heat. You'll need a microwave, some cheesecloth, and double boiler—which is kind of like a saucepan stacked on another saucepan. A cheap candy/deep-frying thermometer is also help-ful, to make sure you keep your concoction at the proper temperature so that too much alcohol doesn't evaporate off. And if you have a gas stove, you'll also need a hot plate, or a friend who doesn't mind you using her electric stove. As we stated emphatically a couple of paragraphs up, *liquor is extremely flamm-mable and you should keep it the hell away from uncontrolled fire.*

Most experts agree that at this point, you need to de-carb the weed. We aren't scientists, so we can't tell you exactly what that means, but long story short, it's a chemistry thing that happens when heat is applied to the dry herb, and it allows all the of amazing, super-fun parts of the THC molecules to bind to the alcohol molecules better. You can heat the weed in a very lowly-lit oven (around 240°F for up to an hour), but we greatly prefer the microwave method pioneered by Warren Bobrow, the author of the excellent, seminal book *Cannabis Cocktails, Mocktails, and Tonics*.

Microwaving weed to de-carb it is not only quick-er and easier, it keeps the weed vibrant and green and imparts much less toasty taste. To microwave your weed, simply place whole buds in a microwave-

safe bowl with a small microwave-safe plate on top of it. Heat for a minute and a half on high, then flip over and turn the buds. Return to the microwave and repeat two more times, turning between, for a total of three spins in the microwave for a minute and a half each. Then, break the weed into small pieces using your fingers or a weed grinder (available at head shops).

How much weed to use depends on how potent you want your infused liquor to be. Jen uses one ⅛-ounce bag for one 750-milliliter bottle of booze, but you can bring that up or down depending on how you want the liquor to taste, how fucked up you want everyone to get, and—of course—how much of your precious herb you're willing to drink rather than smoke.

Be warned, however, that once someone has a marijuana-infused cocktail (especially one of the super-delicious ones we've collected for you in chapter three), they're going to want two, or three. So infuse wisely, and **drink slowly.** Very slowly. Marijuana and alcohol together change the way your body interacts with them, and you might be surprised with how much it effects you—even experienced eaters of edibles say the high is different. We don't recommend drinking weed-infused liquor if you have already been drinking, and if you aren't a regular weed smoker (or eater), you should probably stay away from it entirely. We expect our publisher's lawyers would ask us to tell you to please refrain from using weed at all, and especially **don't buy or consume marijuana anywhere where it is illegal.** (Um, all of our weed-related experiments were totally done at our friend Gary's house in Portland.)

After you've ground your de-carbed weed, it's infusion time! While some experts recommend buying a whipped-cream maker charged by whip-its and using that to rapidly infuse the booze before you heat it, we've found that skipping that weird and expensive step doesn't seem to make a difference…at least, the weed-infused booze we created without it tasted great and worked on all levels.

Fill the bottom half of the double-boiler halfway with water and heat on the electric stove or hot plate it until it starts to boil, at 212°F. Turn the heat to low. In the top half of the boiler, add the bottle of booze of your choice and the ground-up, de-carbed ganj. Stir and cover. If you have a good stove, you can usually leave it on the lowest possible heat setting and let the liquor gently infuse over the next couple of hours. If you have a testy stove, you'll have to watch the alcohol carefully to make sure it doesn't boil, which will start to happen around 170°. (Optimally, you want to keep the liquid in the top of the double boiler at around 150–160°F.) If it does, remove the top part from the heat and turn the heat off, then turn the heat back on after a few minutes. If your stove doesn't go low enough, you may need to alternate between turning the heat off and turning it on low every 5–10 minutes. Luckily, a double boiler keeps the heat consistent on the infusion itself, and after 2 hours you'll have a beautiful, herby spirit full of THC goodness.

Pour the liquor back into its bottle through a funnel with a piece of cheesecloth stretched over the top of it. If some liquor has cooked off, you can add a bit of water or green chartreuse, and no one will ever know. An eighth of an ounce of weed often imparts more of a yellow tone than green, so you might want to add a drop or two of green food coloring for dramatic effect.

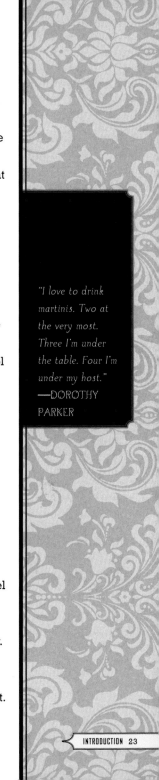

"I love to drink martinis. Two at the very most. Three I'm under the table. Four I'm under my host."
—DOROTHY PARKER

What liquor you infuse is up to you, but our favorite is mezcal, with gin coming in second. This book contains recipes for cocktails that use weed-infused mezcal, gin, whiskey, and spiced rum, as well as some recipes for weed butter, which can be made the same way as weed-infused liquor, but without the de-carbing and with much less time in the double boiler. And of course, we had to include a White Russian with weed-infused cream (page 149) for the Big Lebowski fans. Enjoy, dudes!

PREPARING COCKTAILS

To Shake or to Stir?

Especially if you're going to bother to be one of those people who keeps bitters on hand, the way you prepare cocktails is really important. You can use all the best liquors and freshest mixers, but if you don't know how to make a drink correctly, they're not going to blend together in the right way. Luckily, the rules are pretty simple—it all comes down to whether your drink should be shaken or stirred.

Generally speaking, the most widely accepted rule on shaking vs. stirring is that a cocktail should be shaken when one or more of its ingredients is a juice. Since fruit juice is so dense, shaking it with the alcoholic ingredients ensures a properly mixed and diluted cocktail. Some bartenders (Dylan included) also shake almost all other opaque ingredients. This includes olive juice (for Dirty Martinis) and thick, dense syrups (almond-orgeat, certain types of demerara sugar syrups, etc.). If a cocktail is comprised entirely of alcoholic ingredients, on the other hand, you should stir it (even if the

ingredients are opaque). Stirring drinks that are only comprised of liquor ensures the proper dilution and velvety texture that you want. If you have trouble remembering this, just keep in mind that James Bond was wrong. Ordering an alcohol-based drink like a Martini "shaken, not stirred" is a not only a good way to be an asshole customer, it will leave you with an inferior drink.

If you don't believe us, try shaking a drink that should be stirred, and stirring a drink that should have been shaken. If you shake a Manhattan (page 87), a drink that's supposed to be smooth and spirit-forward, you over-dilute and over-aerate the drink. Meanwhile, if you stir a Margarita (page 125), the ingredients stay somewhat layered, making for an unbalanced drink that changes each time you sip it.

Doing the wrong thing can fuck up your drink, but when you do it right, both stirring and shaking do the same thing. They chill, dilute, and blend the cocktail. By the way—don't worry too much about chilling a cocktail. Shaking doesn't make a cocktail colder than a stirred one. Properly prepared cocktails that are stirred or shaken for fifteen seconds will be cold, we promise.

Special Techniques

Though most of the drinks is this book are super straightforward—shake or stir and then strain into a glass—a few contain some special techniques you should know about.

Muddling is breaking down ingredients like fruits and herbs by pressing them against the side of a glass or shaker with a muddler or pestle.

Floating a liquid on top of a drink means gently pouring it so that it doesn't mix with the heavier liquid below it. (If you can't quite get the hang of it, try placing an inverted spoon over the drink and pouring on top of the spoon, so that the liquid gradually spills off of it.) This is sometimes used in layered shots like the Alice from Dallas (page 47) or for flavor purposes, but it's also used to float a high-proof spirit on top of a drink before you light it on fire, like the Flaming Daiquiri on page 60.

Some of the drinks in this book contain an **absinthe rinse**. This is where you pour a few dashes of absinthe into a glass, then roll it around until the absinthe coats the inside of the glass. This adds a bit of absinthe taste while taking full advantage of its aroma.

LET'S DO THIS

Now that we've armed you with the knowledge to not only make perfect drinks, but to wow everyone around you with liquor facts they never wanted to know, you're ready to make some dangerous cocktails! In chapter one, we'll take you through drinks so delicious you'd hardly know there was booze in them. In chapter two, you'll find classy high-proof cocktails for serious drinkers. And in the last chapter, we'll share our favorite marijuana-based cocktails. Don't forget to check the index if you're looking for a particular drink, or a list of drinks made with each type of alcohol. Enjoy, and drink up!

Chapter 1

DANGEROUSLY EASY TO DRINK

"There's booze in this?!"
Watch out, because these drinks go
down easy—maybe too easy.
Because even though they might
taste like something you'd drink
at a kids' party, the cocktails in
this chapter are decidedly adult…
and more alcoholic than you'd think.

VODKA GIMLET

There's a reason your dad used to knock back three or four of these classy-sounding drinks at every birthday party: they taste just like limeade, but they'll get you pretty drunk, pretty fast. Now you can make them yourself when he comes over. Get drunk together and ask him about the old days!

> 2 ounces vodka
> 1 ounce lime juice
> ¾ ounce simple syrup
> Lime wedge garnish

Shake with ice until cold and blended.
Strain into cocktail glass. Garnish with lime wedge.

LEMON DROP

Pucker up! This drink is super tart, but it's also hard to stop drinking. It's a great on-the-rocks sipper but you can also leave out the ice and drink it as a shooter.

> 1¼ ounces vodka
> ¼ ounce triple sec
> ¼ ounce lemon juice
> Sugar rim
> Lemon peel garnish

Stir with ice until cold and blended.
Strain into cocktail glass with sugared rim.
Garnish with lemon peel.

404

Looking for something with vodka that's not too sweet? You won't err with this refreshing cocktail. The secret ingredient is elderflower liqueur, which makes pretty much any mixed drink taste sophisticated.

1½ ounces vodka
½ ounce elderflower liqueur
¾ ounce lemon juice
½ ounce Aperol
¼ ounce simple syrup
Lemon wheel garnish

Shake with ice until cold and blended.
Strain into cocktail glass. Garnish with lemon wheel.

FRENCH SAILOR

This sweet and warm vodka drink is a sure-thing for warming up sailors lost at sea...as well as French guys who look like they could be sailors.

1½ ounces triple sec, warmed
1½ ounces lemon vodka, warmed
1 sugar cube

Stir warmed triple sec and vodka until well blended. Place sugar cube in old-fashioned glass and slowly pour mixture over it, allowing the sugar cube to dissolve. Gently stir before serving.

CLASSIC COSMOPOLITAN

If you're looking for a fancy drink that still goes down easy, the Cosmo is the drink for you. Plus, it sounds so posh—try *not* doing something weird with your face while saying "Cosmos, anyone?".

　　2 ounces vodka
　　¾ ounce cranberry juice
　　¾ ounce lime juice
　　½ ounce triple sec
　　Lime wheel garnish

Shake with ice until cold and blended.
Strain into cocktail glass. Garnish with lime wheel.

PORN STAR MARTINI

This cocktail contains not only melt-in-your-mouth vanilla syrup, it also has passion fruit juice—one of the best mixers for covering the taste of alcohol. A shot of champagne sipped alongside it takes this sweet elixir to a place so amazing you'll dream of being with it again.

　　2 ounces vodka
　　1½ ounces passion fruit juice
　　5 ounces vanilla syrup
　　½ ounce lime juice
　　2 ounces champagne

Shake all ingredients except champagne with ice until cold and blended. Strain into cocktail glass. Serve alongside a shot glass of champagne.

CHEER UP, DARIA

The only vodka drink he will actually drink, Dylan created this drink for that mopey girl in the corner who you just want to make happy. Once you get her talking, you know she will be tart and spicy with secretly sweet undertones... just like this drink.

1½ ounces vodka
¾ ounce pineapple juice
¼ ounce lime juice
¼ ounce ginger juice
¼ ounce simple syrup
½ ounce spiced
    demerara syrup
Seltzer
Candied ginger and/or
    lime wheel garnish

Shake with ice until cold and blended. Strain into Collins glass with ice. Top with seltzer. Garnish with candied ginger and/or lime wheel.

PARTY PUNCH

CHAMPAGNE SHERBET PUNCH

Go ahead and tell yourself you're making this champagne punch because your grandmother is coming to the party. Secretly, it will be because you can down like ten of these bitches in two hours.

2 quarts lemon sherbet or sorbet, as chilled as possible
5 (750-milliliter) bottles chilled brut champagne
1½ teaspoon Angostura bitters

Place sherbet in punch bowl with ice ring. Pour champagne over sherbet. Add bitters and stir. Refrigerate for 15 minutes before serving.

SOHO MARTINI

Named after Soho resident Lindsay Lohan's dazzling orange hair (nope, just shitting you), this screwdriver with a touch of vanilla is deceptively alcoholic (just like...never mind!).

2 ounces vodka
½ ounce vanilla vodka
½ ounce triple sec
1 dash orange bitters
Flaming orange peel garnish

Stir with ice until cold and blended. Strain into a cocktail glass. Bend orange peel and squeeze over a lit match to ignite its oils. Garnish drink with flaming orange peel.

BANANA SPLIT

This is what we'd call a "dessert drink." Make some of the marijuana cocktails from chapter three with your friends, then serve this decadent cocktail to send them over the edge.

1 ounce vodka
½ ounce banana liqueur
½ ounce Irish cream (classic or caramel)
Cocoa powder rim
Cherry garnish

Shake vodka, crème de bananes, and Irish cream with ice until cold and blended. Strain into martini glass rimmed with cocoa powder. Garnish with cherry.

PEACHES AND CREAM

This sweet and creamy drink will make you feel like you're in a 50s diner with a poodle skirt on. Just make sure you don't drink so many of these that you end up under the booth.

1 ounce vanilla vodka
1 ounce peach schnapps
2 ounces milk

Shake with ice until cold and blended. Strain into cocktail glass.

RASPBERRY SPRITZER

If Jen met Dylan back when she was ordering drinks with raspberry vodka in them, they probably never would have become friends. But you can enjoy this fruity fave of hers even if Dylan wouldn't be caught dead drinking it.

    1½ ounces raspberry vodka
    1 ounce cranberry juice
    2 ounces ginger ale
    Lime wedge garnish

Shake vodka and cranberry juice with ice until cold and blended. Strain into highball glass.
Top with ginger ale and stir.
Garnish with lime wedge.

AMELESS ★★ OOTER ⚡

LE RED CORVETTE

ch of these, then
tire album's
nce songs and
along loudly
ze to no one.

    ¾ ounce orange vodka
    ¼ ounce Aperol
    ¼ ounce lemon juice
    ¼ ounce simple syrup

e until cold and blended. Strain into a shot glass and shoot!

SEX ON THE BEACH

It's safe to say that *none* of us have had as much sex on the beach as we would have liked. Make it all better with the sexiest-named cocktail on Earth.

  1½ ounces vodka
  ½ ounce peach schnapps
  ½ ounce crème de cassis
  1½ ounces orange juice
  1½ ounces cranberry Juice
  Orange wheel garnish

Shake with ice until cold and blended.
Strain into highball glass over ice.
Garnish with orange wheel.

KNOXVILLE LEMONADE

This simple, sunny cocktail allows you to make a fresh, spiked lemonade to your preferred sweetness. Peach schnapps and ginger ale take it to a whole other dimension, and lemon vodka adds a bit more kick. Add more ginger ale in the summer to keep yourself hydrated.

  1 ounce lemon vodka
  1 ounce peach schnapps
  3 ounces lemon juice
  1–3 ounces simple syrup (to taste)
  2 splashes ginger ale
  Orange slice garnish

Shake with ice until cold and blended.
Strain into mason jar over ice.
Garnish with a slice of orange and drink with a straw.

"I began to think vodka was my drink at last. It didn't taste like anything, but it went straight down into my stomach like a sword swallower's sword and made me feel powerful and godlike."
—SYLVIA PLATH

MOVING FJORD

This tart and refreshing Dylan original was created with his cohorts at the Upper East Side's The Gilroy with Purity Swedish Vodka in mind. It's crisp and complex and yes, even pure.

1½ ounces vodka
½ ounce pomegranate liqueur
¾ ounce lime juice
½ ounce pineapple juice
½ ounce almond-orgeat syrup
Grated nutmeg and lime wheel garnish

Shake with small handful of crushed ice until blended. Pour into pilsner glass and fill with additional crushed ice. Garnish with grated nutmeg and lime wheel.

TOM COLLINS

A drink so classic it has a bar glass named after it, a Tom Collins is basically a sparkling gin lemonade. It's best sipped under a tree while Googling the conflicting stories of who Tom Collins was.

1 ½ ounces gin
¾ ounce lemon juice
¾ ounce simple syrup
Club soda
Lemon wheel and/or cherry garnish

Shake gin, lemon juice, and simple syrup with ice until cold and blended. Strain into its eponymous glass over ice. Top with club soda and garnish with a lemon wheel or cherry.

ARMY NAVY

This refreshing classic that goes down as fast as the first day of spring features uniquely flavored almond-orgeat syrup, which gives it a light yet full flavor that gin drinkers will love.

2 ounces gin
½ ounce lemon juice
¼ ounce almond-orgeat syrup
Lemon peel garnish

Shake with ice until cold and blended. Strain into cocktail glass. Garnish with lemon peel.

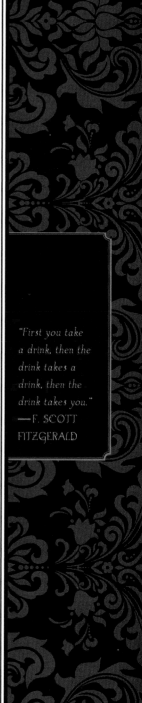

"First you take a drink, then the drink takes a drink, then the drink takes you."
—F. SCOTT FITZGERALD

BEE'S KNEES

. . . .

This drink, Jen's favorite of all time, is ideal for picnics and waiting in line for free outdoor concerts. Just stash some in a chilled thermos and you're ready to go!

> 1½ ounces gin
> ¾ ounce honey
> ½ ounce lemon juice
> Lemon peel garnish

Shake with ice until cold and blended.
Strain into a cocktail glass.
Garnish with lemon peel.

AMELESS★★ ⚡
OOTER ⚡

OYO

. . . .

or the non–gin
art here and
what's not to
he floral herbi-
delicate spirit.

> ¾ ounce gin
> ¾ ounce lemonade
> ¾ ounce grape juice

e until cold and blended. Pour into a shot glass and shoot!

GIN BLOSSOM

We will probably sing along if "Follow You Down" comes on at 3 a.m., but let's be honest, the Gin Blossoms were an embarrassingly mainstream band. This is kind of an embarrassingly mainstream drink, but it's delicious and there's no easier way to drink gin. Plus, it fits in well at any party where the Gin Blossoms would come on at 3 a.m.

1 ounce gin
1 ounce peach schnapps
8 ounces lemon-lime soda like 7-Up

Stir gin and peach schnapps with ice in a cocktail glass (or Solo cup) until cold and blended. Top with soda.

FRENCH 75

Do gin the French way with this classic cocktail. Feel like vodka instead of gin? Then you have a French 76. And if you substitute bourbon, you have a French 95. (We didn't make the rules, we're just telling you them!)

1½ ounces gin
¾ ounce lemon juice
½ ounce simple syrup
Champagne
Lemon peel garnish

Shake with ice until cold and blended.
Strain into champagne flute.
Top with champagne or sparkling wine.
Garnish with lemon peel.

SOUTHSIDE

· ·

**This twist on the gimlet is basically a mojito
with gin instead of rum. They're perfect for
spring drinking—so perfect, in fact, that you'll
want to drink them all through the summer, too.**

2 ounces gin
1 ounce simple syrup
1 ounce lime juice
6 mint leaves
Lime peel garnish

Shake gin, simple syrup, lime juice, and 5 mint leaves
with ice until cold and blended. Fine-strain into
cocktail glass and garnish with remaining mint leaf.

LADY-KILLER

· ·

**Yes, you can still kill with the ladies while drink-
ing a cocktail with fruit juice in it. (It helps if you
have a mustache, though.)**

1 ounce gin
½ ounce triple sec
½ ounce apricot brandy
2 ounces passion fruit juice
2 ounces pineapple juice
Mint sprig garnish

Shake with ice until cold and blended.
Strain into highball glass over ice.
Garnish with mint sprig.

SLOE 75

Sloe gin seems like something your grandpa would drink, but it's actually more of the party girl of spirits thanks to its sweet taste and pink color. This twist on a French 75 isn't particularly boozy, but it gets the job done. Serve it at a bridal shower and the bride's aunts won't know what hit them.

    1 ounce sloe gin
    ½ ounce simple syrup
    ½ ounce lemon juice
    ½ ounce lime juice
    1 dash Angostura bitters
    3 ounces sparkling wine
    Raspberry garnish

Shake all ingredients except sparkling wine until cold and blended. Strain into champagne flute and top with sparkling wine. Garnish with raspberry.

ALABAMA SLAMMER

If you're going to make a cocktail with Southern Comfort, make it a cocktail with a name like the Alabama Slammer. It sounds tough, but goes down easy: this 70s-era classic actually contains just about every sweet spirit currently in your cabinet.

    1 ounce sloe gin
    1 ounce peach liqueur like Southern Comfort
    1 ounce amaretto
    2 ounces orange juice
    Orange wheel and cherry garnish

Shake with ice until cold and blended. Strain into highball glass over ice. Garnish with orange wheel and cherry.

SANTIANNA

Dylan's original twist on a Mezcal Mule is like a more-interesting margarita: delicately layered notes of smoke, sweet, zestiness, and spice. But what really gets it noticed is the flaming cinnamon stick garnish that smokes like incense while you drink it.

1½ ounces mezcal
½ ounce lime juice
½ ounce pineapple juice
½ ounce cinnamon syrup
¼ ounce ginger juice
2 dashes Angostura bitters
Smoking cinnamon stick garnish

Shake with small handful of crushed ice until cold and blended.

Pour into Moscow mule mug. Fill with crushed ice.

Garnish with cinnamon stick. Light cinnamon stick on fire with long lighter, then gently blow out before serving while still allowing to smoke.

NUENA TARDES

This is definitely *not* the drink to give to young children if you're trying to convince them how gross alcohol tastes.

   1 ½ ounces mezcal
   5 ounces apple juice
   1 ounce lemon juice
   Lemon wheel garnish

Shake with ice until cold and blended.
Strain into pint glass. Garnish with lemon slice.

STRAWBERRY BASIL MARGARITA

The addition of strawberries and basil leaves (an odd and beautiful pair) to this traditional margarita adds sweetness and complexity.

   4 strawberries
   4 basil leaves
   ¾ ounce lime juice
   ¾ ounce simple syrup
   1 ½ ounces tequila
   ½ ounce triple sec
   ¼ ounce maraschino liqueur

Muddle 3 strawberries and 3 basil leaves with lime juice and simple syrup. Add remaining ingredients and shake with ice until cold and blended. Strain into margarita glass over ice. Garnish with remaining strawberry and basil leaf.

TEQUILA FRESA

. . . .

**This sweet summer drink is also great blended
with ice and sipped through a straw.**

> 1½ ounces tequila
> ¾ ounce strawberry liqueur
> ½ ounce lime juice
> ½ teaspoon orange bitters
> Strawberry garnish

Shake with ice until cold and blended. Strain into
old-fashioned glass over ice. Garnish with strawberry.

ALAMO SPLASH

. . . .

**The Alamo is a sacred ground where Jan Hooks
explained the many uses for corn while Pee-Wee
was horrified to discover his bike was not in
the basement. Honor it with this fun and fruity
tequila drink.**

> 1½ ounces tequila
> 1 ounce orange juice
> ½ ounce pineapple juice
> Lemon-lime soda, like 7-Up
> Pineapple wedge garnish

Shake all ingredients except soda with ice until cold
and blended. Strain over ice into Collins glass.
Top with splash of 7-Up. Garnish with pineapple wedge.

ALICE FROM DALLAS

We're not sure who Alice is, but we dig her layered shooter. Pour the liquors in the order specified and their varying weights mean the liquids won't blend before you serve this cool-looking shot.

¾ ounce coffee liqueur
¾ ounce orange brandy
¾ ounce tequila

Pour coffee liqueur into chilled shot glass.
Gently float brandy and then tequila on top. Shoot!

PALOMA

If you've ever found yourself stoned at the super-market, wandering the soda aisle and wondering if there's a good drink to make with Squirt, this silly highball is for you. It's also for you if you want a halfway-decent, fizzy margarita that takes about three seconds to prepare!

1½ ounces agave tequila
½ ounce lime juice
5 ounces grapefruit-flavored soda, such as Squirt
Lime wheel garnish

Shake tequila and lime juice with ice until cold and blended.
Strain into highball glass over ice.
Top with soda and stir. Garnish with lime wheel.

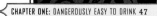

CABALLO

. . . .

The almond-flavored amaretto in this old-school classic gives it a unique taste that you won't forget.

   1½ ounces tequila
   1 ounce amaretto
   6 ounces grapefruit juice
   Lemon peel garnish

Shake with ice until cold and blended.
Strain into Collins glass over ice.
Garnish with lemon peel

WHITE MEXICAN

. . . .

If you like your coffee like you like your men (or women), you'll love this yummy after-dinner drink that tastes like a vanilla iced coffee—but better.

   1½ ounces silver tequila
   ½ ounce coffee liqueur
   1 ounce vanilla cognac
   1½ ounces heavy cream

Shake with ice until cold and blended.
Strain into rocks glass over ice.

COMMODORE

Blended Irish whiskey is great for beginning whiskey drinkers because it's similar to Scotch but much lighter and not so smoky. Add a bit of sweetness, like in this drink, and you'll barely know you're drinking this bold liquor!

- 1¾ ounces Irish whiskey
- 2 teaspoons lime juice
- 1 teaspoon orange juice
- 1 teaspoon strawberry liqueur
- 1 dash orange bitters
- Orange peel garnish

Shake with ice until cold and blended.
Strain into cocktail glass. Garnish with orange peel.

MICHAEL COLLINS

The Michael Collins is our favorite drink named after someone Liam Neeson played in a 90s movie (certainly better than a Rob Roy). It's also crisp and refreshing and perfect for a fall afternoon.

- 1½ ounces Irish whiskey, such as Michael Collins brand
- 2 teaspoons honey
- 1¼ ounces sauvignon blanc wine
- 1½ ounces apple juice
- ¼ ounce lemon juice
- Apple slice garnish

Shake with ice until cold and blended.
Strain into cocktail glass. Garnish with apple slice.

MIA VIDA

Add a pinch of cayenne pepper to add an authentic sweet-yet-spicy kick to this Mexican-inspired iced chocolate.

- 1 ounce tequila
- ½ ounce coffee liqueur
- ½ ounce chocolate liqueur
- ½ ounce heavy cream
- 1 pinch cayenne pepper (optional)
- Grated semi-sweet chocolate garnish

Shake with ice until cold and blended.
Strain into cocktail glass. Garnish with grated chocolate.

SLEEPY HOLLOW

This moody drink by New York bartender Josh Mazza is perfect for Halloween parties and *American Horror Story* marathons. Add a pellet of dry ice to make it truly atmospheric!

- 1½ ounces blended Scotch
- ¾ ounces coffee liqueur
- ½ ounces Ancho Reyes chile liqueur
- 2½ ounces almond milk
- Grated chocolate garnish

Stir with ice until cold and blended. Strain into tiki mug.
Garnish with grated chocolate.

IRISH PENICILLIN

One of Dylan's top five favorite cocktails of
all time (preferably with Powers whiskey),
this light-yet-serious drink by acclaimed
bartender Sam Ross is the perfect cure
for a cough, sore throat, or just a bad day
at work. This twist on the original uses
Irish whiskey instead of blended Scotch.

2 ounces Irish whiskey
1 ounce honey syrup
¾ ounce lemon juice
½ ounce ginger juice
½ ounce Islay Scotch
Candied ginger wheel garnish

Shake Irish whiskey, honey syrup, lemon juice, and ginger juice with ice until
cold and blended. Strain into double rocks glass over ice. Float Scotch on top
and garnish with candied ginger wheel.

IRISH APPLE BOWL

You may know Applejack as a hilarious character in Wes Anderson's debut film *Bottle Rocket*, or an earnest cartoon pony on *My Little Pony: Friendship Is Magic* (or, if you're a bronie, possibly both). But it's also a tasty apple brandy that's featured alongside Irish whiskey in this punch that's more alcoholic than it tastes. Save some lime and apple slices to float on the top as a garnish and serve on Thanksgiving or another autumn occasion.

- 20 ounces Irish whiskey
- 20 ounces applejack
- 7 ounces lime juice
- 3 ounces simple syrup
- 5 dashes orange bitters
- 2 large red apples, sliced thin
- 4 limes, sliced thin
- 2 quarts + 1 pint ginger ale

Pour applejack, whiskey, lime juice, and simple syrup into punch bowl. Add lime and apples. Stir. Refrigerate 1 hour.

Pour in ginger ale and stir. Add large block of ice before serving.

IRISH BLONDE

· ·

Irish whiskey gets a classy upgrade with the help of sherry in this cocktail. Ordering it for an Irish blonde at a bar doesn't guarantee you a date, but it helps!

> **2 ounces Irish whiskey**
> **¾ ounce triple sec**
> **¼ ounce La Ina Fino sherry**
> **1 dash orange bitters**
> **Flaming orange peel garnish**

Stir with ice until cold and blended. Strain into a martini glass. Bend orange peel and squeeze over a lit match to ignite its oils. Garnish drink with flaming orange peel.

CHRISTMAS FIZZ

· ·

Screw the snow, the tree, the elves, and the fat guy, it's not a Christmas party if you haven't had one (or five) of these refreshing cocktails. Multiply this recipe for as many members of your family you're trying to get drunk and serve in the family crystal.

> **1 ounce bourbon**
> **1 ounce cranberry juice**
> **1 ounce cinnamon syrup**
> **2 dashes orange bitters**
> **Seltzer**
> **Cranberry garnish**

Shake bourbon, cranberry juice, cinnamon syrup, and bitters with ice until cold and blended.
Pour into rocks glass over ice. Top with seltzer and stir.
Top with a couple of cranberries.

CINTOSH APPLE

r goes down
apple pie on

1 ounce whiskey
1 ounce apple schnapps
1 splash lemon-lime soda
1 splash cranberry juice

e until cold and blended. Strain into shot glass and shoot!

IRISH NEW YEAR

If you didn't think champagne and whiskey
went together, you've never had this celebratory
cocktail. Watch out, it's hard to drink just one...
or two...or three! If you don't have honey syrup,
simply mix a teaspoon of honey with a half-tea-
spoon of warm water.

1 ounce Irish whiskey
½ ounce lemon juice
¼ ounce honey syrup
1 ounce sparkling wine
Lemon peel garnish

Shake whiskey, lemon juice, and honey syrup with ice
until cold and blended. Strain into champagne flute.
Top with sparkling wine and stir.
Garnish with a twisted lemon peel.

CRANBERRY-RUM COOLER

Rum is a common ingredient in punches and coolers because it really shines with fruit, and this cocktail recipe featuring Christmassy cranberry juice is no exception.

- **1 ounce light rum**
- **1 ounce dark rum**
- **4 ounces cranberry juice**
- **2 ounces orange juice**
- **½ ounce lemon juice**
- **Lemon wedge garnish**

Shake with ice until cold and blended.
Strain into a Collins glass over ice.
Garnish with lemon wedge.

★★ SHAMELESS SHOOTE

WHISKEY SOUR JELL-O SH

There is a time and a place for Jell-O shots. When you come to that time and place, here's the recipe you need.

- **1 (3-ounce) package gelati dessert powder**
- **1 ½ ounces whiskey**
- **¾ ounce lemon juice**

Prepare gelatin dessert according to package directions, redu water by ⅓ cup and substituting whiskey and lemon juice inste
Pour into paper or plastic shot cups before setting in refrigera
Pop out and shoot!

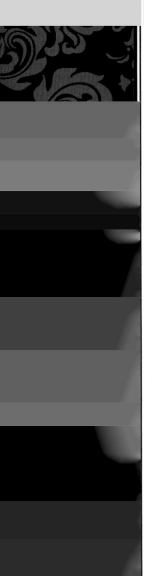

FRAT HOUSE

This one's for you, bros: because we want you to have a way to enjoy that Everclear that doesn't make us shake our heads in embarrassment. This drink basically tastes like a bathtub Dark 'n' Stormy...but that doesn't mean you should actually make it anywhere near your bathtub.

> **2 ounces grain alcohol like Everclear**
> **5 ounces root beer**
> **1 ounce lemon juice**

Stir with ice in old-fashioned glass (or Solo cup) with ice until cold and blended.

STONE FENCE

Although rums made from sugarcane have become more popular in recent years, traditional molasses-based rums have a sweet, almost caramel-tasting undertone that make them a natural fit for fall cocktails like this one.

> **2 ounces rum (preferably molasses-based)**
> **2 dashes Angostura bitters**
> **Fresh apple cider**
> **Lemon wheel and grated nutmeg garnish**

Stir with ice in a double-rocks glass. Top with apple cider. Stir. Garnish with lemon wheel and grated nutmeg.

CATEGORY FIVE HURRICANE

In New York, we don't batten down the hatches when a hurricane is coming, we shut down the subway and hole up with a cocktail party–sized hoard of booze. If you're in a similar situation, make sure to pick up some passion fruit juice before you hit the long line at the grocery store so you can sip this tiki classic while the city blows down.

2 ounces light rum
2 ounces dark rum
2 ounces passion fruit juice
1 ounce lime juice
1 ounce orange juice
½ ounce grenadine
½ ounce simple syrup
Lime wheel garnish

Shake all ingredients with ice until cold and blended. Strain into hurricane glass with ice. Garnish with lime wheel.

BOLO

A mimosa for drunks, this is the ideal drink for when you're wavering between still being drunk from the prior night and starting to get a hangover. Rum replaces the champagne, while simple syrup and lemon juice add more depth to give this easy-to-prepare cocktail a sophistication that will make you feel better about having a completely unproductive weekend.

1½ ounces light rum
½ ounce lemon juice
½ ounce orange juice
¼ ounce simple syrup
Lemon slice garnish

Shake with ice until cold and blended.
Strain into cocktail glass. Garnish with lemon slice.

DERBY RUM FIX

This variation on the Bolo is a perfect brunch drink on Kentucky Derby Day or any other spring morning.

2 ounces light rum
½ ounce lime juice
1 ounce orange juice
¼ ounce simple syrup
Orange slice garnish

Shake with ice until cold and blended.
Pour into highball glass. Garnish with orange slice.

PARTY PUNCH

JUNGLEBIRD

It doesn't get more punchy than this bittersweet 70s classic.
If you want a traditional, fruity punch that everyone will
drink five glasses of before they realize how drunk they are,
this is the party drink for you.

7½ ounces dark rum
7½ ounces pineapple juice
2½ ounces Campari
2½ ounces lime juice
2½ ounces simple syrup
Pineapple and lime wheel garnishes

In a series of shakers, add ingredients and shake until cold and blended.
Strain into punch bowl with large ice cubes. Serve in old-fashioned
glasses garnished with pineapple and lime wheels.

MALIBU BAY BREEZE

We don't like to use the term "girly drink,"
but let's face it, this is a girly drink...a delicious
girly drink that goes down easier than Kool-Aid.

1½ ounces coconut rum
2 ounces cranberry juice
2 ounces pineapple juice
Pineapple wedge garnish

Shake with ice until cold and blended.
Pour into highball glass. Garnish with pineapple wedge.

FLAMING DAIQUIRI

Rum, fresh lime juice, and simple syrup is a flawless combination, but let's face it: it's not particularly exciting until you float overproof rum on top and light it on fire. Go for the guts and the glory in this daiquiri with a flaming float.

1½ ounces light rum
¾ ounce simple syrup
1 ounce lime juice
Lime half garnish
1 ounce overproof rum

Shake rum, simple syrup, and lime juice with ice until cold and blended. Strain into cocktail glass. Carefully float overproof rum on top and light with long lighter. Let burn off before serving. Hollow out lime half, then carefully float it on top of drink. Fill with overproof rum and light on fire. Let burn out before serving.

MOJITO

This classic Cuban cocktail is what you want to be drinking the second you get off of work on the first day of spring. Just be warned: they're so good you should probably make a pitcher.

5 mint leaves
1½ ounces light rum (preferably sugarcane-based)
¾ ounce lime juice
¾ ounce simple syrup
1½ ounces club soda
Mint sprig and/or sugarcane garnish

Muddle 5 mint leaves. Add rum, lime juice, and simple syrup. Shake with ice until cold and blended. Pour into highball glass and add additional ice if necessary. Top with club soda. Garnish with stick of sugarcane and/or mint sprig.

BLUE HAWAIIAN

Perhaps because of its bright color, blue curaçao seems to find its way into a lot of homemade cocktail experiments...and "experiments" is being charitable. If you're tempted to buy that big blue bottle when you come across it at the liquor store, make some Blue Hawaiians, which are delightfully fruity without being weird.

1½ ounces light rum
1½ ounces blue curaçao
3 ounces pineapple juice
1 ounce cream of coconut
Pineapple wedge and/or cherry garnish

Shake well with ice. Pour into Collins glass. Garnish with pineapple wedge and/or cherry.

AMER

MING ZOMBIE

the few ways you can
by lighting it on fire.
the flaming version
ki drink by floating
on top, then lighting
serving. Make an
ah, whatever" face
g the drink with a
blowing out the flames.

1 ounce light rum
1 ounce dark rum
1 ounce lime juice
1 ounce lemon juice
1 ounce pineapple juice
1 teaspoon brown sugar
1 dash Angostura bitters
1 ounce overproof rum
Mint sprig garnish

ents except overproof rum with ice until cold and blended.
ane glass over crushed ice. Float overproof rum on top and
long lighter. Blow out and garnish with mint sprig.

APPLE SAZERAC

If you love maple syrup, you have to try this wintery
twist on a Sazerac! Make it even more impressive
by stirring it with snow rather than ice…assuming
you live somewhere where your snow isn't dirty by
the time it hits the ground.

2 ounces apple brandy
¼ ounce maple syrup
3 dashes Peychaud's bitters
Lemon wheel garnish

Stir with ice until cold and blended.
Strain into old-fashioned glass. Garnish with lemon wheel.

SHOOTER

BUTTERY NIPPLE

It's not as much fun as a *real* buttery nipple, but nothing much is.

1 ounce butterscotch schnapps
½ ounce Irish cream

Shake with ice until cold and blended. Strain into shot glass and shoot!

SPIKED CHAI ICED TEA

What's better than a Chai Iced Tea in the summer? A Spiked Chai Ice Tea! This drink is also how Jen celebrated Manhattan's decriminalization of public drinking. It's the only to enjoy the city streets in true style.

- 14 ounces brewed chai tea, chilled
- 2 ounces Irish cream
- 1 ounce heavy cream
- 1 ounce simple syrup
- Dash cinnamon syrup

Shake with ice until cold and blended. Strain into a clean, 24-ounce (medium) plastic cup from your favorite coffee shop over ice. Drink with a straw.

FLAMING DR. PEPPER

Did you know that Amaretto and overproof rum lit on fire and slammed into a beer tastes just like a foamy Dr. Pepper? If you don't believe us, try it. (And if you do believe us, we know you're already halfway to the fridge.)

¾ ounce Amaretto
¼ ounce overproof rum
8 ounces pilsner beer

Pour Amaretto into shot glass and float overproof rum on top. Light on fire and drop into half-full glass of pilsner. Slam it!

TOASTED ALMOND

You may know amaretto from sickly sweet Amaretto Sours, but this pairing with coffee liqueur and cream brings out its silky almond flavor and it allows it to be the pleasing accent it should be rather than the main attraction.

- 2 ounces Amaretto
- 2 ounces coffee liqueur
- 2 ounces light cream

Shake with ice until cold and blended.
Strain into rocks glass over ice, if desired.

"All I ever did was supply a demand that was pretty popular."
—AL CAPONE

PISCO PUNCH

Pisco, a piquant brandy made with grapes, is the national spirit of Peru. It's showcased well in this classic cocktail that's gratifyingly sweet-yet-sour.

- 2 ounces Pisco brandy
- 2 ounces pineapple juice
- 1 ounce lime juice
- 1 ounce simple syrup
- Pineapple wedge and cherry garnish

Shake with ice until cold and blended.
Strain into a white wine glass over ice.
Garnish with pineapple wedge and cherry.

Chapter 2

DANGEROUSLY BOOZY

The super-alcoholic drinks we've mixed up in this chapter are mostly made with high-proof liquor— but high-proof doesn't have to mean hot and hootchy. Instead, these concoctions for serious drinkers bring out the intense flavors of the liquor while perfectly balancing them.

NAVY NEGRONI

Legend has it that this bittersweet cocktail is named for an Italian Count—but all you need to know is that Negronis are fucking delicious and boozy and hell. This version uses (naturally) navy strength gin to make it even boozier.

- 1 ounce navy strength gin
- 1 ounce sweet vermouth
- 1 ounce Campari
- Orange peel garnish

Stir with ice until cold and blended.
Strain into double-rocks glass with ice.
Garnish with orange peel.

NORTHPOINT NEGRONI

This take on a Negroni was created by Nati Rabinowitz, a fellow regular at one of our favorite Brooklyn bars. He uses Contratto Bitter rather than Campari to give this drink a more complex, slightly less sweet taste.

- 1 ounce navy strength gin
- 1 ounce Contratto Bitter
- 1 ounce grapefruit juice
- Lemon wedge garnish

Shake with ice until cold and blended.
Strain into cocktail glass.
Garnish with squeezed lemon wedge

THE MAGRITTE

We named this boozed-up twist on a traditional drink called the Marguerite after *Art of Living* painter Rene Magritte. Did we get too highfalutin for you? OK, just drink a few of these, and you'll feel like your head is a giant orange.

   2 ounces navy strength gin
   1 ounce dry vermouth
   1 dash orange bitters
   Orange peel garnish

Stir well with ice until cold and blended.

Strain into martini glass.

Garnish with lemon peel

LUCIEN GAUDIN

It's easy to make a drink that's pure booze, but making one that's pure booze and also classy as hell is a bit harder. The Lucien Gaudin combines navy strength gin with three stand-up standbys (triple sec, Campari, and vermouth), and it's so posh it's even hard to pronounce!

   1 ounce navy strength gin
   ½ ounce triple sec
   ½ ounce Campari
   ½ ounce dry vermouth
   Orange peel garnish

Stir with ice until cold and blended.

Strain into cocktail glass.

Garnish with orange peel.

NAVAL MARTINI

This drink doesn't fuck around! A martini made with high-proof gin, it will pistol whip you into happy hour and won't apologize.

2½ ounces navy strength gin
¾ ounce dry vermouth
3 dashes orange bitters
Lemon peel or olive garnish

Stir with ice until cold and blended. Strain into cocktail glass. Garnish with lemon peel or olive.

ENSIGN MARTINEZ

Believe it or not, the Martinez preceded its famous (and dryer) cousin the Martini into the world. Legend has it that it was created by a bartender on a ship that sailed regularly between the Californian cities of San Francisco and Martinez. The martini was later invented as a riff on the popular drink.

- 2 ounces navy strength gin
- 1 ounce sweet vermouth
- ¼ ounce maraschino liqueur
- 2 dashes orange bitters
- 2 dashes Angostura bitters
- Orange peel garnish

Stir with ice until cold and blended.
Strain into cocktail glass. Garnish with orange peel.

HANKY PANKY

This classic twist on the Martinez with a navy-strength boost replaces the maraschino with fernet—a dark and herby liqueur from Italy. Serve with a shot of straight fernet if it's after 2 a.m.

- 1½ ounces navy strength gin
- 1½ ounces sweet vermouth
- ¼ ounce fernet
- Orange peel garnish

Stir with ice until cold and blended.
Strain into cocktail glass.
Garnish with orange peel.

TUXEDO

This funky, fancy martini is perfectly balanced, so you might not notice that you're basically drinking booze + bitters. If you really want to make it dangerous, substitute navy strength gin for the regular stuff.

1½ ounces gin
1½ ounces dry vermouth
¼ ounce maraschino liqueur
2 dashes absinthe
3 dashes orange bitters
Orange peel garnish

Stir with ice until cold and blended.
Strain into cocktail glass. Garnish with orange peel.

BREAKFAST IN BROOKLYN

If you find yourself in Brooklyn on a Sunday morning, having toast and jam with a couple of ladies, make them this drink. And don't be surprised if everyone ends up back in bed, in a good way.

2 ounces navy strength gin
¾ ounce lemon juice
¾ ounce triple sec
¼ ounce simple syrup
1 bar spoon strawberry preserves
Strawberry garnish

Shake with ice until cold and blended.
Fine-strain into cocktail glass. Garnish with strawberry.

GIN-GIN MULE

Ginger tastes so fantastic in cocktails that there's a name for them: mules. This simply delicious mule uses gin and mint to highlight its zesty ginger taste.

2 ounces navy strength gin
¾ ounce simple syrup
¾ ounce lime juice
½ ounce fresh ginger juice
2 dashes Angostura bitters
6 fresh mint leaves,
    plus 1 sprig for garnish
Seltzer

Shake with ice until cold and blended.
Strain into Collins glass with ice
and top with seltzer.
Garnish with mint sprig.

ABIGAIL SPONDER

This take on the Sazerac from Francis Verrall of The Gilroy became a fave of Dylan's and the rest of the bartenders there. We prefer it with Old Tom gin's Spring44 and Carpano Antica Formula vermouth.

> 1 ounce gin
> 1 ounce cognac
> ¾ ounce sweet vermouth
> ¼ ounce Cointreau Noir
> 3 dashes Peychaud's bitters
> 2 dashes orange bitters
> Lemon peel garnish

Stir with ice until cold and blended.

Rinse double rocks glass with absinthe.

Strain into glass without ice. Garnish with lemon peel.

BLACKTHORN

This classic drink made with Dubonnet (an aperitif) and Kirschwasser (a deliciously sour—not sweet—cherry liqueur) is supposedly a favorite of Queen Elizabeth's. It's probably unbefitting of a queen to quaff more than a couple of drinks, so luckily just two of these should put her to bed for the night!

> 2 ounces navy strength gin
> ¾ ounce Dubonnet Rouge
> ¾ ounce Kirschwasser
> Lemon peel garnish

Stir with ice until cold and blended.

Strain into cocktail class. Garnish with lemon peel

VALENTINE'S KISS

This original cocktail from New York bartender JJ Condon is easily the nicest drink in this book. This kiss is sealed with cherry heering, a dark and delicious cherry brandy.

2 ounces navy strength gin
½ ounce yellow chartreuse
½ ounce cherry heering
Lime zest garnish

Stir with ice until cold and blended.
Strain into coupe glass. Zest lime over top for garnish.

FLAMING MOE

If you've ever wondered what the secret ingredient in a Flaming Moe/Flaming Homer was, it was a bit of mezcal thrown in with whatever else Homer had handy that night. (And even if you don't get the *Simpsons* reference, you're still allowed to drink our take on this legendary flamer.)

¼ ounce gin
¼ ounce vodk
¼ ounce light
¼ ounce mezc
¼ ounce triple
¼ ounce blue
1 dash sweet a
1 dash cranbe
2 dashes over

Stir gin, vodka, rum, mezcal, and triple sec with ice until co
Strain into hurricane glass over ice. Add sour mix and cran
stir. Add blue Curaçao and stir until drink becomes purple.
rum on top. Light on fire, then blow out before serving.

CORPSE REVIVER #2

Yes, there is a **Corpse Reviver #1**, but no one ever makes it. This twist on the popular #2, which features the floral Lillet Blanc aperitif, uses navy strength gin for even more necromantic properties.

¾ ounce navy strength gin

¾ ounce triple sec

¾ ounce Lillet Blanc

¼ ounce absinthe

¾ ounce lemon juice

Lemon peel garnish

Shake with ice until cold and blended. Strain into cocktail glass. Garnish with lemon peel.

PLEAD THE 5th

If your significant other asks you tomorrow, you don't remember pounding back these shooters.

¾ ounce navy strength gin
¾ ounce white Sambuca
¾ ounce coffee liqueur

Shake with ice until cold and blended. Strain into shot glass and shoot!

VESPER

Although James Bond really should have had his martinis stirred, we can give him props for inventing the Vesper. (Or at least, Ian Fleming did, in his novel *Casino Royale*.) Though 007 used Gordon's gin, we know he would have approved of something stronger.

3 ounces navy strength gin
1 ounce vodka
½ ounce Lillet Blanc
Lemon peel garnish

Stir with ice until cold and blended.
Strain into cocktail glass. Garnish with lemon peel.

MORNING PRAYER

Jen doesn't usually go to church, but if she does, she drinks this cocktail that Dylan created for just such a purpose. A twist on the Vesper that highlights the vodka rather than gin (less booze on your breath!), it also features Dimmi, a delicate peach-blossom liqueur from Italy that's hard not to fall in love with.

1½ ounces vodka
½ ounce navy strength gin
½ ounce Dimmi liqueur
¼ ounce Lillet Blanc
¼ ounce yellow chartreuse
2 dashes celery bitters
Lemon peel garnish

Stir with ice until cold and blended.
Strain into cocktail glass.
Garnish with lemon peel.

OAXACA MARTINI

Named after the home of mezcal, Oaxaca, and created by bartender Caleb Mayes, this martini also contains Lillet, a unique-tasting apertif that blends beautifully with yellow chartreuse and mezcal.

1½ ounces mezcal
¾ ounce Lillet Blanc
¾ ounce yellow chartreuse
Lemon peel garnish

Stir with ice until cold and blended.
Strain into cocktail glass. Garnish with lemon peel.

ROMAN CANDLE

This drink, which Dylan created at Brooklyn's Bar Chord, balances clove-y Velvet Falernum with smoky mezcal and bright grapefruit bitters for an afterhours cocktail with a distinct taste.

1½ ounces mezcal
¾ ounce dry vermouth
½ ounce Velvet Falernum
3 dashes grapefruit bitters
Lemon peel garnish

Stir with ice until cold and blended.
Strain into cocktail glass. Garnish with lemon peel.

TKO

This drink isn't strong enough to leave you on the ground—just strong enough to make your brain a dizzy mess so that technically, you might as well be on the ground. It also makes a great shooter if you decrease the amount and get rid of the ice.

1¼ ounces mezcal or tequila
1¼ ounces coffee liqueur
1¼ ounces Ouzo

Stir with ice until cold and blended.
Strain into cocktail glass over ice.

AMELESS ★★
OOTER

) HOT

nokiness of
the sharpness
in this spicy
natural
n.

¼ ounce mezcal
¾ ounce cinnamon schnapps

e until cold and blended. Strain into shot glass and shoot!

DEADBOLT

When we start mixing up Deadbolts, shit is going down.
We prefer to use Ilegal Mezcal Joven and to party Oxacan style.
Use Cynar 70 for even more of a kick.

- 1¼ ounces mezcal
- 1¼ ounces blended scotch
- ½ ounce Velvet Falernum
- ½ ounce Cynar
- 2 dashes chocolate bitters
- Lemon peel

Stir with ice until cold and blended. Strain into double rocks glass.
Express oils from lemon peel into drink and discard.

REMEMBER SCOTLAND

This classy and complex drink by New York bartender JJ Condon is best enjoyed while reminiscing with your old crowd. A twist on the Remember the Maine (page 97), it uses smoky Scotch from the Islay region.

> ¾ ounce Islay Scotch
> ¾ ounce Suze
> ½ ounce dry vermouth
> ½ ounce sweet vermouth
> ½ ounce cherry heering
> Lemon zest and brandied cherry garnish

Stir with ice until cold and blended. Strain into coupe glass. Garnish with lemon zest and brandied cherry.

MORNING GLORY FIZZ

You might find egg whites in drinks gross in theory, but they're not there for flavor (or for protein). Although you can't taste them, they add a delightful foaminess that in drink parlance is often called a "fizz." Use a pasteurized egg, as consuming unpasteurized raw eggs can be dangerous (and not in a good way).

> 2 ounces bonded Scotch
> 1 teaspoon Pernod liqueur
> ½ ounce lemon juice
> ¼ ounce simple syrup
> ½ of an egg white from 1 pasteurized egg
> 1 dash Peychaud's bitters
> Club soda
> Lemon wheel garnish

Shake with ice until cold and blended.
Strain into highball glass. Add splash of soda and enough ice to fill. Stir. Garnish with lemon wheel.

"Scotch whisky is made from barley and the morning dew on angel's nipples."
— *WARREN ELLIS*

BOURBON DAISY

You might have thought we were just being flowery, but a "daisy" is actually a drink that mixes club soda and something sour (in this case, lemon juice). Grenadine, a popular bar syrup made from pomegranates, adds a touch of sweetness, and a Southern Comfort float makes it downright dangerous.

- 1½ ounces bonded bourbon
- ½ ounce lemon juice
- 1 teaspoon grenadine
- Club soda
- 1 bar spoon Southern Comfort
- Orange peel garnish

Shake bourbon, lemon juice, and grenadine with ice until cold and blended. Strain into highball glass filled halfway with ice. Add soda and stir. Float Southern Comfort on top. Garnish with orange peel.

BOURBON COLLINS

If you want to be one of those badasses who just sips their bourbon on the rocks, but you're just not quite there yet, try a Bourbon Collins. This classic take on a Tom Collins adds a touch of sweet-and-sour complexity to an average bourbon and soda.

- 2 ounces bonded bourbon
- 2 dashes Peychaud's bitters
- ½ ounce lemon juice
- ¼ ounce simple syrup
- Club soda
- Lemon slice garnish

Shake with ice until cold and blended. Strain into Collins glass filled halfway with ice. Top with soda and stir. Garnish with lemon slice.

STMAS IN THE CITY

. . . .

want a flaming
for Christmas, we
vhat your problem is.
illed with absinthe
oated on top of a spicy,
sed cocktail that has a
blate thanks to some
hing-for molé bitters.

1 ounce bourbon
1 ounce cognac
½ ounce triple sec
2 dashes orange bitters
2 dashes molé bitters
Clementine half garnish
½ ounce absinthe

on, cognac, triple sec, and bitters with ice until cold and
ain into cocktail glass. Hollow-out half of a Clementine,
absinthe and float on top. Light absinthe on fire.
before serving.

BOULEVARDIER

. . . .

**Back before the internet, hipsters had to have zines
to voice their fervently held beliefs about everything
from awesome music to things you should totally
drink. In 1920s Paris, an American expat who was
surely a hipster had a zine called the *Boulevardier*,
which published this drink, a twist between a
Manhattan and a Negroni.**

1½ ounces bonded bourbon
½ ounce Campari
½ ounce sweet vermouth
1 dash Angostura bitters
Lemon peel garnish

Stir with ice until cold and blended.
Strain into cocktail glass. Garnish with lemon peel.

KENTUCKY BUCK

In the drinks world, a mule is a cocktail made with ginger, and a buck is a mule that doesn't use a white spirit like vodka or mezcal. This version is perfect for Derby Day or any day you've been doing some bucking.

2 ounces cask strength bourbon
¾ ounce lemon juice
¼ ounce simple syrup
¼ ounce ginger juice
Mint sprig garnish

Shake with ice until cold and blended. Strain into copper mug and fill with crushed ice. Garnish with mint sprig.

SERMON ON THE BARREL

Dylan won a fancy award for this sweet and herbal drink that's like mesquite barbecue in a glass. The secret ingredient is wood vinegar—make sure you get the food-grade kind and not the pesticide! This drink is as intense as a preacher going off about hellfire, but it isn't *pesticide* dangerous. Treat yourself to a nice bonded bourbon for this drink; we prefer Elijah Craig 12 Barrel Proof.

1½ ounces bonded bourbon
¾ ounce Suze
¾ ounce Dubonnet Rouge
¼ ounce Bénédictine
2 dashes food-grade wood vinegar
Orange peel garnish

Stir with ice until cold and blended. Strain into double rocks glass with ice. Garnish with orange peel.

THE CLOSE TALKER

This original take on the Rob Roy was named after the *Seinfeld* character for a reason: after you down this powerful cocktail people might be smelling it on your breath all night.

> 1¼ ounces bonded bourbon
> ¾ ounce Islay Scotch
> ½ ounce sweet vermouth
> ½ ounce Cynar 70
> 3 dashes Angostura bitters
> Orange peel garnish

Stir with ice until cold and blended.

Strain into double rocks glass.

Garnish with orange peel.

★★ SHAMELESS ★★ SHOOTER ⚡

TOUCH OF FRENCH

Amaretto and Irish cream form a sweet and creamy topping for bonded bourbon in this layered shooter.

> ½ ounce bourbon
> ¼ ounce Amaretto
> ¼ ounce Irish cream

Pour whiskey into shot glass. Stir amaretto and Irish cream with ice until cold and blended. Pour over whiskey to float. Shoot!

TRADER'S MANHATTAN

The whole point of drinking rye with a higher
alcohol concentration isn't to get you drunk faster
(unlike overproof rum which, let's be honest, is
for parties). It's to be able to more easily taste the
notes in the spirit unique to that cask. A Manhattan
is the consummate way to taste and enjoy bonded
rye. Just make sure to stir, not shake!

  2 ounces bonded rye
  1 ounce sweet vermouth
  3 dashes Angostura bitters
  Brandied cherry garnish

Stir with ice until cold and blended.
Strain into cocktail glass. Garnish with brandied cherry.

OLD OSCAR

This original cocktail by Francis Verrall features
spicy Ancho Reyes chile liqueur alongside delicious
Amaro Montenegro, an increasingly popular Italian
spirit that's infused with more than forty herbs and
spices. It's relatively low proof, and has notes of
rose pedal and honey that will make you want to
add it to just about every cocktail you make.

  1½ ounces bonded bourbon
  ½ ounce Ancho Reyes chile liqueur
  ½ ounce Amaro Montenegro
  ½ ounce Campari
  3 dashes chocolate bitters
  Orange peel garnish

Stir with ice until cold and blended. Strain into double
rocks glass with ice. Garnish with orange peel.

TRADE WINDS

A relative of Amaro Montenegro, Averna Amarao is a touch darker, and contains notes of baking spices, chocolate, and peppercorns. Add a few drops of cold brew coffee and herby Suze and you have a strong complement to a strong spirit: white corn whiskey. For this original drink, we actually prefer a Mellow Corn whiskey—which is both the name of a distillery and an apt description for their 100-proof yellow whiskey that's aged, but only for four years.

- 1½ ounces Mellow Corn whiskey
- ¾ ounce Suze
- ½ ounce Averna Amaro
- ¼ ounce simple syrup
- 3 drops cold brew coffee
- 2 dashes chocolate bitters
- Orange peel garnish

Stir with ice until cold and blended. Strain into cocktail glass with no ice. Garnish with orange peel.

WINTER IS COMING

This bracing drink uses white corn whiskey, which is bourbon that hasn't been aged. Corn whiskeys from most national brands taste terrible, but if you happen upon a local distillery that makes small batches, pick up a bottle and enjoy its super-bright taste with this simple cocktail.

- 2 ounces white corn whiskey
- 1 ounce triple sec
- 1 ounce ginger juice
- 1 dash orange bitters
- Orange peel garnish

Shake with ice until cold and blended.
Strain into martini glass. Garnish with orange peel.

RYE ITALIAN

This cocktail will make you think of pizza—but not one of those late-night slices you'd pile chili flakes on—one of those delicately balanced fancy pizzas that remind you of that summer you spent in Italy. It features saba, a sweeter relative of balsamic vinegar, which makes the drink both sweet and tart. If you can't find it, you can use balsamic vinegar that's been reduced by half instead.

- 1½ ounces bonded rye
- ¾ ounce lemon juice
- ½ ounce simple syrup
- 1 bar spoon saba (grape must syrup)
- Basil leaf garnish

Shake with ice until cold and blended.
Strain into rocks glass over ice. Garnish with basil leaf.

RED HOOK

Maybe because it's hard to get to by train, but Red Hook is a neighborhood in Brooklyn where adventures seem to happen. This spin on the Manhattan has a similar touch of mysterious sweetness, while still feeling familiar.

2 ounces bonded rye
½ ounce sweet vermouth
½ ounce maraschino liqueur
Orange peel garnish

Stir until cold and blended.
Strain into cocktail glass.
Garnish with orange peel.

VALKYRIE

This softer version of a Manhattan, served down (that is, without ice) contains Averna Amaro as well as St. Germain, a liqueur made from elderflowers that makes everything light, lovely, and delicious.

2 ounces bonded rye
½ ounce Cynar
½ ounce Averna Amaro
¼ ounce elderflower liqueur
2 dashes grapefruit bitters
Lemon peel garnish

Stir with ice until cold and blended.
Strain into double rocks glass.
Garnish with lemon peel.

JUNGLE JUICE

Nobody in their right mind should make this party punch. But if it's Spring Break and you happen to have six or seven bottles of booze sitting around, don't you kind of owe it to all of us to head to the store for some pineapple juice and limes? This original recipe is by Dylan who (it must be said) is from Orlando, the Spring Break capital of the world.

1 (1-liter) bottle grain alcohol like Everclear
1 (5-liter) bottle vodka
1 (750-milliliter) bottle peach schnapps
2 (750-milliliter) bottles dark rum
1 (1-pint) bottle overproof rum
4 quarts pineapple juice
4 quarts lime juice
½ quart simple syrup
2 (12-ounce) cans ginger ale
6 (12-ounce) cans pilsner beer
Slices of pineapple, kiwi, watermelon, pears, or whatever fruit is available

Pour all ingredients into cooler with spout over ice (we recommend opening all 6 cans of beer at once and pouring while still attached to the six-pack). Add fruit slices. Let sit for 2 hours before serving. Drink before cops are called.

ACONDA

uca is a flavorful relative of absinthe that is perfectly
whiskey in this dangerous-sounding shooter.

bonded bourbon or rye
white Sambuca

ntil cold and blended. Strain into shot glass and shoot!

FINAL WORD

**Green chartreuse goes so well with weed-infused
liquors that we saved most our drink recipes
featuring it for the final chapter (Dangerous, with
Drugs). But this sweet 'n' sour 'n' spicy twist on
the Last Word (see page 118) drunk without a
garnish is so simple and perfect that we had to
keep it pure.**

- **¾ ounce bonded rye**
- **¾ ounce lemon juice**
- **¾ ounce green chartreuse**
- **¾ ounce maraschino liqueur**

Shake with ice until cold and blended.
Strain into cocktail glass.

THE LIBERAL

Don't accuse us of getting all political—the Liberal first appeared in the 1895 book *Modern American Drinks* by Gabe Kapler. The original featured an amari called Amer Picon that has gone extinct. We've replaced it here with the similar Amaro Ciociaro from Italy.

> 1¾ ounces bonded rye
> ¼ ounce sweet vermouth
> ¼ ounce Amaro Ciociaro
> 2 dashes orange bitters
> Orange peel garnish

Shake with ice until cold and blended.

Strain into cocktail glass and garnish with orange peel.

★★S H A M E L E S S
SHOOTER

ONE-EYED RYE

This isn't a shooter, it's a straight-up shot. Get a chaser handy because this turned-up version of the One-Eyed Rye is going to feel as bad as it does good.

¾ ounce overproo[f]
¾ ounce bonded r[ye]
Lemon wedge

Stir with ice until cold and blended. Strain into shot glass and
with lemon wedge. Shoot!

VIEUX CARRÉ

This old New Orleans cocktail is almost as old as the Sazerac, to which it's quite similar. The addition of sweet vermouth and Bénédictine not only gives you a reason to go rooting around at the back of your cabinet for those liquors grandpa left you, it leads to a more complex cocktail.

  1 ounce bonded rye
  1 ounce cognac
  1 ounce sweet vermouth
  ¼ ounce Bénédictine
  2 dashes Peychaud's bitters
  2 dashes Angostura bitters
  Orange peel garnish

Stir with ice until blended and cold. Strain into double rocks glass over ice. Garnish with orange peel.

LA LOUISIANE

Another classic twist on the Sazerac, this cocktail really lets the herbal, sweet, and aromatic wonderfulness of Bénédictine shine. You'll be amazed at how sippable it is if you've only ever had it in stuffy B&B (which Jen once owned a bottle of for five years before it got drunk at a party that had run out of booze).

  2 ounces bonded rye
  ¾ ounce sweet vermouth
  ¾ ounce Bénédictine
  3 dashes absinthe
  3 dashes Peychaud's bitters
  Brandied cherry garnish

Stir with ice until cold and blended.
Strain into cocktail glass. Garnish with brandied cherry.

SERIOUS SAZERAC

Give this serious drink some respect: the Sazerac is the oldest cocktail that's still served in bars today. Like the ancient spirits it's comprised of, it was originally medicine—developed at a New Orleans apothecary in the 1840s by none other than Mr. Peychaud himself, Antoine Amedie, who also created the famous bitters. Like the original, this version rinses the glass with absinthe, giving it a bigger aroma *and* more medicinal properties.

4 dashes absinthe
1½ ounces bonded rye
1½ ounces cognac
½ ounce simple syrup
4 dashes Peychaud's bitters
2 dashes Angostura bitters
Lemon peel garnish

Add absinthe to double rocks glass and rotate to rinse glass with absinthe. Stir remaining ingredients with ice until cold and blended. Strain into glass. Garnish with lemon peel.

BLUE BLAZER

Perhaps the first flaming cocktail ever invented and still the most dangerous, the Blue Blazer was invented by father of the cocktail Jerry Thomas and is named for the tunnel of blue flame that travels from one mug to another after you light this simple cocktail and start mixing it. We do *not* recommend wearing gloves made out of asbestos when preparing this drink, as some bartenders originally did after it appeared in Thomas' original bartenders' guide. However, we *do* recommend wearing Ove Gloves or any other Ove Glove–like product you bought off the TV, just so you don't accidentally burn the shit out of your hands. Only perform this mixing trick with thick, heavy steel mugs with flared rims that make pouring from one to the other easy. Clear away any flammable materials, and have a fire extinguisher handy! Do a few trial runs with water before attempting with whiskey, and consider that maybe your skills just don't lie in pouring liquids and you should not attempt this crazy-dangerous drink at all. Lay down a sliver platter (as Thomas originally suggested), or just lots of damp towels in case of spills. Roll up your sleeves. You know what? Don't make this drink at all. But here's how to do it, for historical purposes only. One more thing, dim the lights. Yes, really, you'll be able to see the flames better.

> 6 ounces bonded whiskey
> ½ ounce honey syrup
> Lemon peel garnish

Heat whiskey in microwave in 10–15 second increments until warmed. Add honey syrup to one mug and whiskey to the other. Light whiskey on fire with long lighter. Carefully pour the contents of each mug of whiskey back and forth between the mugs, creating a blue stream. When flames subside pour into two crystal goblets and garnish with lemon peel.

SEA CAPTAIN'S SPECIAL

Both whiskey and absinthe were used as medicine before they were used recreationally, and this drink from the 1940s was said to help sea-sickness. These days, it's more often used as a hangover cure (thanks to the sugar and the bubbles), making it the absolute best drink to serve on a booze cruise.

> Sugar cube
> 1 dash club soda
> 3 dashes Angostura bitters
> 2 ounces bonded rye
> 1½ ounces champagne
> 2 dashes absinthe

Place sugar cube in old-fashioned glass and wet with club soda and bitters. Muddle until dissolved, then rotate glass to spread mixture evenly. Add small amount of ice and add rye, then champagne, then absinthe to glass

REMEMBER THE MAINE

This historic cocktail with an absinthe rinse is sweet and dangerous, appropriate for a drink named after the rallying cry ("Remember the *Maine*, to Hell with Spain!") that helped start the Spanish-American war.

> 3 dashes absinthe
> 2 ounces bonded rye
> ¾ ounce sweet vermouth
> ¼ ounce cherry heering
> ¼ ounce cherry brandy
> Lemon peel garnish

Add absinthe to cocktail glass and rotate to rinse glass with absinthe. Stir remaining ingredients with ice until cold and blended. Strain cocktail into glass. Garnish with lemon peel.

TRUST FUND

Add bonded rye to a Boulevardier—which is a word for a socialite, but also a tasty drink that's essentially a Negroni with rye instead of gin (see page 84)—and you have a Trust Fund. Drink a few of these before you crash an upscale party and you'll have the guts to smile at the bouncer as you strut on by.

1½ ounces bonded rye
¾ ounce sweet vermouth
¾ ounce Campari
Orange slice garnish

Stir with ice until cold and blended.
Strain into double rocks glass with ice.
Garnish with orange slice.

OLD PAL

This take on a Boulevardier is for those who prefer a dryer cocktail...and probably a dark corner of a neighborhood bar to drink it in. Using dry instead of sweet vermouth also allows the Campari to shine through, and the end of your sip will have much more rye flavor.

1½ ounce bonded rye
¾ ounce Campari
¾ ounce dry vermouth

Stir with ice until cold and blended.
Strain into cocktail glass. Garnish with orange peel.

MORNING GLORY

What's the story, Morning Glory? In this case, it's a bubbly classic that mixes natural companions rye and cognac with absinthe.

1 ounce bonded rye
1 ounce cognac
¼ ounce simple syrup
¼ ounce absinthe
2 dashes Angostura bitters
Seltzer
Lemon peel garnish

Stir rye, cognac, simple syrup, absinthe, and bitters with ice until cold and blended. Strain into double rocks glass with ice. Top with seltzer. Garnish with lemon peel.

"A man's got to believe in something. I believe I'll have another drink."
—W. C. FIELDS

DANGEROUS DARK AND STORMY

. . . .

A Dark and Stormy is one of those drinks that is done often, but often not done right. This version uses ginger juice rather than ginger beer (an important component of those drinks in the "done right" category), an aged rum float for flavor, overproof rum to make sure it has enough kick, and an elegant garnish: a candied wheel of ginger. Enjoy.

> **1 ounce overproof rum**
> **½ ounce simple syrup**
> **¾ ounce lime juice**
> **½ ounce fresh ginger juice**
> **1 ounce black rum**
> **Candied ginger and lime garnish**

Shake all ingredients except black rum with ice until cold and blended. Strain into Collins glass with ice. Top with seltzer. Pour black rum over seltzer, floating it on top. Garnish with candied ginger and lime.

CUBA LIBRE

. . . .

Don't drink an extra-boozy Rum and Coke, drink a *Cuba Libre*—it sounds cooler. A 1-to-2 rum-to-Coke ratio is standard, but use less Coke the more hardcore you are.

> **2 ounces overproof rum**
> **4 ounces cola**
> **Lime wedge garnish**

Stir with ice until cold and blended in rocks glass. Garnish with lime wedge.

GET LIIT

This Long Island Ice Tea will get you Liit...with two *i*s. (It's also an acronym, get it?). Though it doesn't contain any high-proof liquor, it contains pretty much every liquor except whiskey.
Cola adds a tea-like color that gives it the name that somehow lends it a bit of respectability.

¾ ounce rum
¾ ounce vodka
¾ ounce gin
¾ ounce tequila
¾ ounce triple sec
¾ ounce lemon juice
Cola
Lemon wheel garnish

Pour all ingredients into hurricane glass with crushed ice. Stir. Top with cola. Garnish with lemon wheel.

★★ SHAMELESS ★★ SHOOTER ⚡

LIQUID COCAINE

Ah Jägermeister and Goldschläger. They sound so sophisticated, yet somehow they ended up the mascots of out-of-hand college students who you just wish would go to sleep. But since they make up a shooter known as "Liquid Cocaine," they deserve to be in this book. Enjoy!

¼ ounce overproof rum
¼ ounce Jägermeister
¼ ounce Goldschläger
¼ ounce pineapple juice

Stir with ice until cold and blended. Strain into shot glass and shoot!

NUCLEAR DAIQUIRI

Velvet Falernum is a liqueur from Barbados that's too mysterious to describe, except maybe to say "clove-y." Pair it with green chartreuse and lime juice and you get an even more mysterious taste, with an odd greenish-yellowish hue that gives this drink its nuclear color. Overproof rum, meanwhile, gives it its nuclear strength.

> 1 ounce overproof rum
> ¾ ounce green chartreuse
> 1 ounce lime juice
> ¼ ounce Velvet Falernum
> Lime wheel garnish

Shake with ice until cold and blended.
Fine-strain into cocktail glass. Garnish with lime wheel.

SUPERMAN'S KRYPTONITE

If you have a bunch of random-ass liquors in your cabinet when Halloween or St. Patrick's Day rolls around, you'll be excited to know that you have the perfect ingredients to make this bright-green cocktail. And even if your friends would normally not be caught dead drinking Malibu and Midori, on holidays no rules apply!

> 1½ ounces spiced rum
> 1½ ounces coconut rum
> 1½ ounces melon liqueur like Midori
> 1 ounce overproof room
> 1½ ounces pineapple juice

Stir with ice until cold and blended.
Strain into cocktail glass.

PARTY PUNCH

FISH-HOUSE PUNCH

The fish-house in question when it comes to boozy punch isn't some sort of tuna factory or late-night Congee place. It's a swanky Philadelphia gentleman's club so old-school that George Washington is said to have drunk this punch there. Legend has it that it is so potent that George was unable to write in his diary for three days afterward.

1 (750-milliliter) bottle golden rum
1 (750-milliliter) bottle spiced rum
1 (750-milliliter) bottle cognac
6 ounces peach-flavored brandy
24 ounces lemon juice
6 ounces simple syrup
24 ounces seltzer

Add all ingredients to punch bowl and stir. Refrigerate for 1 hour. Add large chunk of ice before serving.

JET PILOT

This high-proof tiki classic is plenty of jet fuel to keep you flying all night.

1¾ ounces dark rum
¾ ounce overproof rum
½ ounce grapefruit juice
½ ounce lime juice
½ ounce cinnamon syrup
1 dash Angostura bitters
6 dashes absinthe
Brandied cherry and lime wheel garnish

Shake with ice until cold and blended.
Strain into hurricane glass over ice.
Garnish with brandied cherry and lime wheel.

TI' PUNCH

. . . .

If you're having a few people over and you just want to have a classy, non-fruity punch for adults, this is the one for you. Swapping out regular white rum and simple syrup for sugarcane-based rum and a spiced syrup made from demerara sugar (that brown "raw sugar") elevates this drink to something simple yet complex and perfectly balanced.

> 10 ounces sugarcane-based rum
> 1 ounce spiced demerara syrup
> 5 ounces lime juice

Pour into punch bowl. Add large pieces of ice and stir. Let sit for 30 minutes and stir again before serving.

PIÑA COLADA ON THE ROCKS

. . . .

If you're on a fake beach in Vegas and somebody offers you one of those blended Piña Coladas that seem to stick to the roof of your mouth, go ahead and take one. But if you're going to make one yourself, do yourself a favor and make it on the rocks. Use coconut milk rather than the thick cream of coconut used in most recipes, and add a couple of dashes of bitters to balance out the sweetness that usually hits you on the back of the throat.

> 1 ounce light rum
> 1 ounce coconut rum
> ½ ounce overproof rum
> 1½ ounces coconut milk
> 2½ ounces pineapple juice
> 2 dashes Angostura bitters
> Pineapple wedge garnish

Shake with ice until cold and blended. Pour into hurricane glass over ice. Garnish with pineapple wedge.

CARIBOU LOU

Not all drinks invented by rappers are good, but this deconstructed Piña Colada attributed to TECH N9NE is so simple and without fault that the fact it has its own rap seems beside the point.

> 1½ ounces overproof rum
> 1 ounce coconut rum
> 4 ounces pineapple juice

Shake with ice until cold and blended.
Pour into rocks glass over ice.

AUNT ROBERTA

According to unsubstantiated internet rumors, this dark red and delicious concoction was named by a raccoon trapper after a beloved late-and-great bar owner/moonshine maker from Alabama. The story is too good to look into the truth behind it!

> 1 ounce absinthe
> 1½ ounces vodka
> ½ ounce overproof rum
> 1 ounce brandy
> ¾ ounce gin
> ½ ounce blackberry liqueur
> Blackberry garnish

Pour all ingredients into double rocks glass over ice. Stir. Garnish with blackberry.

ABSINTHE WITHOUT LEAVE

This shooter featuring fruity Dutch liqueur Pisang Ambon has a cool layered look and a witty name. What more do you need?

¾ ounce absinthe
¾ ounce Irish cream
¾ ounce Pisang Ambon

Pour absinthe into shot glass. Float cream liqueur and Pisang Ambon on top. Shoot!

BANKS' CADAVER

Before gin was the light and crisp spirit we know today, it was genever, an ancient juniper berry–based spirit from the Netherlands and Belgium that takes center stage in this JJ Condon original. Usually found in the US under the Bols brand, genever is a malty, almost-sweet spirit that's perfectly balanced in this drink with elderflower, bittersweet Campari, and a hint of absinthe.

3 dashes absinthe
1½ ounces genever
¾ ounce Campari
¾ ounce elderflower liqueur
Orange zest garnish

Stir until cold and blended.
Strain into coupe glass.
Garnish with orange zest.

DEATH IN THE AFTERNOON

Enjoying absinthe doesn't have to involve a ton of other liquors and mixers. Sometimes, it's as simple as layering some bubbly on top of it and sipping at your leisure. Perfect for afternoon drinking *après* a morning full of mimosas, it was supposedly one of noted lush Ernest Hemingway's favorites.

1 ounce absinthe
Champagne
Lemon peel garnish

Pour absinthe into champagne flute.
Top with champagne.
Garnish with lemon peel.

ABSINTHE DAIQUIRI

We prefer Plantation brand rum in this extra-boozy yet easy-to-make daiquiri that also contains absinthe.

2 ounces dark rum
1 ounce lime juice
¾ ounce simple syrup
3 dashes absinthe
Pinch salt
Lime peel garnish

Shake with ice until cold and blended.
Strain into cocktail glass. Garnish with lime peel.

FLAMER

ABSINTHE DRIP

One of the most fun things ever to do with a sugar cube, this classic absinthe preparation gave us the absinthe spoon— and possibly freebasing.

¼ ounce absinthe
½ ounce simple syrup
Sugar cube

Set a sugar cube on an absinthe spoon over a glass. Soak sugar cube with absinthe and light on fire. Let it burn for a few seconds and douse with simple syrup. Dissolve rest of cube with more absinthe.

TRIDENT

If you've been to Iceland, you probably know about its signature spirit, Brennivin, a.k.a. "Black Death," an unsweetened schnapps made from potatoes and a secret mixture of Icelandic herbs. It tastes a little bit like licorice, and like most secret spirits of small countries, ex-pats who try it claim it can have hallucinogenic properties. We love it in this take on a classic.

1 ounce Brennivin
1 ounce Cynar 70
1 ounce sherry
Brandied cherry garnish

Stir with ice until cold and blended.
Strain into cocktail glass. Garnish with brandied cherry.

B2C2

Legend has it that American soldiers from World War II invented this highly drinkable (and highly alcoholic) cocktail as a manly way to drink a huge store of French booze that the Nazis had left behind after the their defeat.

1½ ounces brandy
1½ ounces Bénédictine
1½ ounces triple sec
Brut champagne

Stir brandy, Bénédictine, and triple sec with ice until cold and blended. Strain into old-fashioned glass.
Top with champagne.

Chapter 3

DANGEROUS, WITH DRUGS

If you've ever wondered what combining your love of booze and your love of weed into a classy cocktail would be like, you're going to love this chapter. Weed-infused liquor forms the base of these drinks, which have an herbal aftertaste and "edibles" edge. Make sure to see pages 20–24 for a quick how-to and some important safety warnings before you dig in.

WAKE 'N' BAKE

This weed-infused version of a Breakfast Martini is the quintessential drink for those wake 'n' bake brunches. Aromatic Bénédictine ups the ante on the weed flavor while the lemon juice and grapefruit bitters add a bright acidity. Everything is pulled together perfectly by the secret ingredient, sweet citrus marmalade.

> 1½ ounces weed-infused gin
> ½ ounce Bénédictine
> ¾ ounce lemon juice
> 2 bar spoons citrus marmalade
> 2 dashes grapefruit bitters
> Lemon peel garnish

Shake with ice until cold and blended.
Strain into cocktail glass. Garnish with lemon peel.

SMOKIN' SIDECAR

If you love sour strains of marijuana, you'll love this take on a classic Sidecar, another New Orleans original that was made famous during Prohibition.

> 2 ounces weed-infused gin
> 1 ounce triple sec
> 1 ounce lemon juice
> Flaming lemon peel garnish

Shake with ice until cold and blended.
Strain into old-fashioned glass. Bend lemon peel and
squeeze over a lit match to ignite its oils.
Garnish drink with flaming lemon peel.

GIN AND JUICE

This classic cocktail is usually called **Gin and Sin**, but this weed infusion will make you think only of smoking endo, laid back. Try to keep your mind off your money and your money off your mind.

> 1½ ounces weed-infused gin
> 1 ounce orange juice
> 1 ounce lemon juice
> 1 teaspoon grenadine
> Lemon peel garnish

Shake with ice until cold and blended.
Strain into cocktail glass. Garnish with lemon peel.

PARTY PUNCH

WE SAIL AT DAWN

The weed-free version of this drink was created by Dylan at The Gilroy, where he makes his own oleo saccharum by vacuum-sealing sugar along with lemon and orange peels to make a highly concentrated syrup that's like simple syrup, except with citrus oil rather than water. You, however, can buy some on the internet.

10 ounces weed-infused gin
10 ounces earl grey tea
5 ounces oleo saccharum
2½ ounces green chartreuse
Lemon peels garnish

Add all ingredients to punch bowl and stir until blended. Add large ice cubes. Garnish with lemon peels.

OLD FLAME

. . . .

If you love the taste of orange, you'll love this fancy cocktail with weed-infused gin that's topped with (appropriately) a flaming orange peel.

> **1 ounce weed-infused gin**
> **½ ounce sweet vermouth**
> **¼ ounce Campari**
> **½ ounce triple sec**
> **1½ ounces orange juice**
> **Flaming orange peel garnish**

Shake with ice until cold and blended. Strain into cocktail glass. Bend orange peel and squeeze over a lit match to ignite its oils. Garnish drink with flaming orange peel.

A M E L E S S ★ ★
OOTER

NKA

. . . .

**r is a nice way to enjoy the flavor of weed-infused gin
ing to drink it straight.**

> **eed-infused gin**
> **orange bitters**
> **green chartreuse**

Stir with ice until cold and blended. Strain into shot glass and shoot!

CLAYTON BIGSBY

Basically a weed-infused White Negroni, this is the perfect cocktail to drink while enjoying reruns of *Chappelle's Show*. Suze adds extra herbiness while Lillet adds lightness to the weed-infused gin.

> 1 ounce weed-infused gin
> 1 ounce Suze
> 1 ounce Lillet Blanc
> Lemon peel garnish

Stir with ice until cold and blended.
Strain into cocktail glass over ice.
Garnish with lemon peel

FLYING HIGH

Based on an Aviation, this favorite cocktail of Dylan's is a fantastic showcase for crème de violette—a dry, floral liqueur that tastes like boozy rose water. It hits all the right notes with maraschino liqueur (use Luxardo) and weed-infused gin.

> 2 ounces weed-infused gin
> ½ ounce lemon juice
> ½ ounce maraschino liqueur
> ¼ ounce crème de violette
> Lemon peel garnish

Shake with ice until cold and blended.
Fine-strain into cocktail glass. Garnish with lemon peel.

CHAPTE

GREEN DRAGONFLY

. . . .

"Green Dragon" is the name often given to weed-infused liquor of any kind. This cocktail with weed-infused gin actually tastes great with any kind other type of pot-infused liquor. Try it with infused mezcal!

   1½ ounces weed-infused gin
   3 ounces ginger ale
   Lime wedge garnish

Pour into rocks glass over ice. Stir.
Garnish with lime wedge.

TWENTIETH CENTURY

. . . .

This fun, contemporary classic features our favorite apertif, Lillet Blanc, and has a hint of cocoa thanks to the white crème de cacao.

   1½ ounces weed-infused gin
   ¾ ounce Lillet Blanc
   ½ ounce white crème de cacao
   ¾ ounce lemon juice
   Lemon peel garnish

Shake with ice until cold and blended.
Strain into cocktail glass. Garnish with lemon peel.

BIJOU

Ask them what they'd pair weed-infused spirits with and most bartenders immediately think of green chartreuse. Besides giving your infusion a little extra boost of green, it has an herbal element that pairs perfectly with reefer. Drink it in this cocktail and you'll see how funny the word "Bijou" sounds when you say it stoned.

1 ounce weed-infused gin
1 ounce green chartreuse
1 ounce sweet vermouth
2 dashes orange bitters
Lemon peel garnish

Stir with ice until cold and blended.
Strain into cocktail glass.
Garnish with lemon peel.

LAST WORD

The Last Word is another classic cocktail that, thanks to its green chartreuse, goes perfectly with weed-infused gin. This is an especially lovely mixer if you've infused your gin with a strain that has citrusy undertones.

¾ **ounce weed-infused gin**
¾ **ounce green chartreuse**
¾ **ounce maraschino liqueur**
¾ **ounce lime juice**

Shake with ice until cold and blended. Strain into cocktail glass

THE THIRD STATE

Alaska may have been the forty-eighth state to enter the Union, but it was the third state to make recreational use of marijuana legal. Celebrate with the weed-infused version of a classic called the Alaska, which features yellow chartreuse, a great pairing for weed-infused gin.

2 ounces weed-infused gin
¾ ounce yellow chartreuse
2 dashes orange bitters
Lemon peel garnish

Stir with ice until cold and blended.
Strain into cocktail glass.
Garnish with lemon peel.

MINTY MORNING

The only thing that goes with mint better than gin is weed. Have them all together in another drink that's great for waking and baking.

2 sprigs fresh mint
1½ ounces weed-infused gin
½ ounce lemon juice
¼ ounce simple syrup

Lightly muddle mint in old-fashioned glass.
Shake remaining ingredients with ice until cold and blended.
Pour over mint. Stir.

WATERMELON LIMEADE

Nothing says "I'm serious about partying" like a punch bowl literally made out of a watermelon. Take this weed-infused punch over the top by using a watermelon-flavored beer like the 21st Amendment Brewery's Hell or High Watermelon.

12½ ounces weed-infused gin
12½ ounces watermelon juice
3¾ ounces lime juice
2½ ounces simple syrup
12 ounces wheat beer, preferably watermelon-flavored

In a series of shakers, add all ingredients except beer and shake until cold and blended. Strain into a hollowed-out half watermelon. Add large ice cubes. Top with watermelon-flavored beer. Garnish with lime wheels and mint sprigs.

WHITE GIRL

It's not a White Lady, it's a White Girl—which
means there's a rim you can also snort.
(We don't actually suggest snorting Pixy Stix.
But keep this drink in mind for a wild party.)

   2 ounces dry gin
   ½ ounce triple sec
   ½ ounce lemon juice
   Orange-flavored Pixy Stix rim

Stir with ice until cold and blended. Pour into cocktail
glass with Pixy Stix rim. Garnish with rolled up dollar bill.

GANJA NEGRONI

Showcase some delicious weed-infused mezcal
with sweet vermouth and Campari in this
classic cocktail.

   1½ ounces weed-infused mezcal
   ¾ ounce sweet vermouth
   ¾ ounce Campari
   Orange slice garnish

Stir with ice until cold and blended.
Strain into double rocks glass over ice.
Garnish with orange slice.

UP ALL NIGHT

A Tequila Sunrise with weed-infused mezcal, this bright drink with a sharp edge is *the* drink for seducing stoners who are also surfers or lifeguards. Just make sure to do it in your beach bungalow and not where anybody can drown.

> 1½ ounces weed-infused mezcal
> ½ ounce lime juice
> 4 ounces chilled orange juice
> 1 teaspoon grenadine
> Lime wedge garnish

Shake with ice until cold and blended.
Pour into rocks glass. Garnish with lime wedge.

MEZCAL MIEL

The grapefruit and honey in this spin on a mule bring a sweet and sour taste to smoky, herby weed-infused mezcal. The perfect afternoon drink!

> 1½ ounces weed-infused mezcal
> ½ ounce honey liqueur
> 4 ounces grapefruit juice
> Grapefruit peel garnish

Shake with ice until cold and blended.
Strain into rocks glass over ice.
Garnish with grapefruit peel.

NAKED AND FAMOUS

The weed-free version of this contemporary classic is attributed to bartender Joaquin Simo at Pouring Ribbons in the East Village. Not only is it our photographer's fave, but the yellow chartreuse pairs beautifully with the infused mezcal.

- ¾ ounce weed-infused mezcal
- ¾ ounce yellow chartreuse
- ¾ ounce Aperol
- ¾ ounce lime juice

Shake with ice until cold and blended. Strain into cocktail glass.

MINTED MEZCAL

Smoky mezcal and fresh mint are brought together with herby marijuana in this stimulating cocktail. Hand it to your guests as soon as they get to your barbecue and it will immediately be the best they've ever attended.

- 6 large mint leaves
- 1½ ounces weed-infused mezcal
- ½ ounce lemon juice
- ¼ ounce simple syrup
- Mint sprig garnish

Lightly muddle mint leaves at bottom of old-fashioned glass. Shake remaining ingredients with ice until cold and blended. Pour over mint. Stir. Garnish with mint sprig and additional bud, if you're feeling generous.

PROSPECT PICNIC

A picnic in Brooklyn's Prospect Park isn't complete until someone sneaks into the trees to smoke a joint. Get high without having to take a break from Wiffle Ball with this refreshing summer drink featuring weed-infused mezcal and Aperol, an orangey Italian spirit. (And if you're playing Wiffle Ball without a drink in your hand, you're doing it wrong.)

  1 ounce weed-infused mezcal
  ¾ ounce Aperol
  ½ ounce maraschino liqueur
  ¾ ounce lime juice
  Lemon peel garnish

Shake with ice until cold and blended.
Strain into coupe glass. Garnish with lemon peel.

ULTIMA PALABRA

The kava-kava root is from the South Pacific and is said to have psychedelic properties. Infuse some in a bottle of mezcal the same way you would weed to make this cocktail (Spanish for its namesake, the Last Word) and it will leave you flying.

  ¾ ounce kava-kava infused mezcal
  ¾ ounce green chartreuse
  ¾ ounce maraschino liqueur
  ¾ ounce lime juice

Shake with ice until cold and blended.
Strain into cocktail glass.

MAGIC DRAGON MARGARITA

Mezcal and marijuana—a smoky, herby combination you won't soon forget after tasting it. Like Cinco de Mayo and Four-Twenty all rolled into one, this festive fuckery of a drink is perfect for parties.

2 ounces weed-infused mezcal
1 ounce lime juice
¾ ounce triple sec
½ ounce simple syrup
Lime wheel garnish

Shake with ice until cold and blended. Strain into double rocks glass rimmed with salt (if desired) and filled with ice. Garnish with lime wheel and, if you're feeling generous, extra bud.

CAPITAN ROMERO

This original cocktail tastes almost Christmassy with its combination of rosemary and lemon. Add weed-infused mezcal and you get the distinct taste of the Christmas tree burning down (in a good way!).

1½ ounces weed-infused mezcal
¾ ounce Aperol
½ ounce lemon juice
½ rosemary syrup
Rosemary sprig garnish

Shake with ice until cold and blended.
Strain into cocktail glass. Garnish with rosemary sprig.

BLOODY MARIA

Want to know the secret to a great Bloody Maria (the mezcal version of a Bloody Mary)? Celery salt. Oh, and weed.

1½ ounces weed-infused mezcal
2 ounces tomato juice
1 teaspoon lemon juice
1 dash hot sauce
1 dash celery salt
Lemon slice garnish

Shake until blended and strain into an old-fashioned glass with ice. Garnish with lemon slice.

PETROLEUM

This shooter, a deconstructed Bloody Maria, will definitely help fuel your morning.

1 ounce weed-infused mezc
2 dashes hot sauce
2 dashes Worcestershire sau
1 dash lemon juice

Shake with ice until cold and blended. Strain into shot glass a

LIT-UP LEMONADE

You're a stoner alcoholic smuggling booze onto the beach in a giant cooler with a spout. What do you make? This Lit-Up Lemonade, of course (simply multiply the recipe by four or five). Just don't drink and swim, folks. In fact, maybe keep this whole thing to your backyard lawn chair or neighbor's barbecue.

2 ounces weed-infused Scotch
1 tablespoon lemon juice
½ ounce simple syrup
½ ounce grenadine
Lemon-lime soda, like 7-Up
Lemon slice garnish

Shake with ice until cold and blended.
Strain into Collins glass over ice. Top with soda.
Garnish with lemon slice.

CHRONIC CLIQUET

· ·

"Cliquet" means "ratchet" in French, but there's nothing ratchet about this classic and classy cocktail.

> 1½ ounces weed-infused whiskey, preferably bourbon
> 1 teaspoon dark rum
> 2 ounces orange juice
> Orange wheel garnish

Shake with ice until cold and blended.

Strain into rocks glass. Garnish with orange wheel.

AMELESS ★★
OOTER ⚡

ZY IZZY

· ·

r was dizzy
en added
ke sure to
feet after
e back.

1 ounce weed-infused Scotch
1 ounce sherry
2 dashes lemon juice
2 dashes pineapple juice

e until cold and blended. Strain into shot glass and shoot!

DERBY DAY MINT JULEP

Guess what goes perfectly with a classic Kentucky Derby Mint Julep? If you said weed, you're one step ahead of us on this delicate infusion of mint and marijuana.

10–12 fresh mint leaves
2½ ounce weed-infused bourbon or rye
¾ ounce simple syrup
Mint sprig garnish

Pack julep mug with 10–12 fresh mint leaves. Add whiskey and crushed ice. Add simple syrup and more crushed ice. Garnish with mint sprig. Serve with lit joint.

MUSHROOM HOT TODDY

Mushrooms, like the ancient spirits whiskey and absinthe, have always had a tradition rooted in medicine. Whatever mushrooms you decide to imbibe (of course, we officially advocate only the safe and legal ones, for holistic purposes), you can make a tea with them and then add them to a hot toddy with ginger and lemon for maximum healing benefits.

2 ounces bourbon
¼ ounce fresh ginger juice
¾ ounce lemon juice
1 ounce honey syrup
3 dashes Angostura bitters
4 ounces mushroom-infused hot water

Add bourbon, ginger juice, lemon juice, honey syrup, and bitters to mug and stir. Add mushroom-infused hot water and stir again. Sip slowly.

REVOLVER

Attributed to San Francisco bartender Jon Santer, this contemporary classic with a Mary-Jane spin combines coffee liqueur with spicy bourbon and a hint of orange.

   1¼ ounces weed-infused bourbon
   ½ ounce coffee liqueur
   2 dashes orange bitters
   Orange peel garnish

Stir with ice until cold and blended.
Strain into a cocktail glass. Garnish with orange peel.

COLONEL KUSH

If you love sweet tea (and weed), you won't be able to get enough of this drink, based on a Cool Colonel. Brew a strong batch of black tea and chill in the fridge before assembling, and make sure to multiply the recipe by as many as you plan to drink on the beach.

   1½ ounces weed-infused bourbon
   1 ounce Southern Comfort
   3 ounces chilled black tea
   2 teaspoons lemon juice
   ½–1 ounce simple syrup (to taste)
   Club soda

Shake all ingredients except club soda with ice until cold and blended. Strain into Collins glass over ice. Add splash of club soda and stir.

MONK'S CURE

This weed-infused twist on a Monte Carlo gets its name from Bénédictine, a great herby complement to weed-infused liquor that was first developed by monks in the 1500s.

   1 ½ ounces weed-infused bourbon
   ¾ ounce Bénédictine
   1 dash Angostura bitters

Stir with ice until cold and blended.
Strain into cocktail glass.

NIGHTSHADE

Nightshade is a poisonous plant that, like whiskey and marijuana, was used in ancient medicines. It can also be what happens when you decide to tell your late-night drinking companions exactly what you think of them. The best nightshade, however, is this complex and herby cocktail, infused with weed.

   1 ½ ounces weed-infused bourbon
   ½ ounce sweet vermouth
   ½ ounce orange juice
   ¾ ounce yellow chartreuse
   Flaming orange peel garnish

Stir with ice until cold and blended. Strain into old-fashioned glass. Bend orange peel and squeeze over a lit match to ignite its oils. Garnish drink with flaming orange peel.

RYE HIGH

This take on an Old-Fashioned, one of the earliest cocktails ever written down, is a simple way to enjoy weed-infused bourbon or rye.

2 ounces weed-infused bourbon or rye
¼ ounce simple syrup
3 dashes Angostura bitters
Orange peel garnish

Stir until cold and blended. Strain into double rocks glass over ice. Garnish with orange peel.

ACCIDENTAL HIPSTER

The name of this Chris and Julia Tunstall original was invented before the drink itself—the thought being that a drink could contain so many "in" ingredients that you could become a hipster after drinking it. If such a drink exists, this one certainly fits the bill—especially when you use weed-infused rye.

¾ ounce weed-infused rye
¾ ounce fernet
¾ ounce maraschino liqueur
¾ ounce lemon juice
Lemon peel garnish

Shake with ice until cold and blended.
Strain into cocktail glass. Garnish with lemon peel.

NEW YORK SOUR DIESEL

Sour Diesel is a classic sativa strain native to New York City, just like a New York Sour. Bring them together and you have this drink, a weed-infused whiskey sour with a red wine float.

> 2 ounces weed-infused
>   bourbon or rye
> 1 ounce lemon juice
> ¾ ounce simple syrup
> 1 egg white from a pasteurized egg
> 1 ounce red wine

Shake whiskey, lemon juice, simple syrup, and egg white dry (without ice), then add ice and continue to shake until cold and blended. Strain into cocktail glass. Gently pour red wine on top to float.

PEYOTE

• •

This sweet-and-sour gem is a weed-infused
version of the vintage Algonquin cocktail, which is
supposedly named after the Manhattan hotel that
was made famous as a Prohibition-era stomping
grounds for writers like Dorothy Parker and F. Scott
Fitzgerald. If they were around today, we think
they'd enjoy our weed-infused version.

> 1½ ounces weed-infused rye
> 1 ounce dry vermouth
> 1 ounce pineapple juice
> 2 dashes orange bitters

Stir with ice until cold and blended.
Strain into cocktail glass.

TORONTO

• •

Dark and mysterious fernet liqueur is paired
with weed-infused rye in this take on the classic
cocktail.

> 2 ounces weed-infused rye
> ¼ ounce fernet
> ¼ ounce simple syrup
> 2 dashes Angostura bitters
> Orange peel garnish

Stir with ice until cold and blended.
Strain into cocktail glass. Garnish with orange peel.

TNT

. . . .

Pastis is a French cousin of absinthe. It pairs beautifully with weed-infused rye in this herby, spicy shooter that will make you shiver.

1 ounce weed-infus
1 ounce Pastis

Stir until cold and blended. Strain into shot glass and shoot!

SFV

. . . .

SFV is a laid-back strain of kush from the San Fernando Valley. Infuse it into some rye and serve it in this cocktail based on the San Francisco and you'll feel downright Californian.

2 ounces weed-infused rye
¼ ounce Bénédictine
¾ ounce lemon juice
2 dashes Angostura bitters
Lemon slice garnish

Shake with ice until cold and blended.
Strain into cocktail glass. Garnish with lemon slice.

TIPPERARY

Here's another green chartreuse and grass pairing, this one featuring Irish whiskey along with sweet vermouth. Watch out, it's strong!

- 1½ ounces weed-infused Irish whiskey
- ¾ ounce sweet vermouth
- ½ ounce green chartreuse
- Orange peel garnish

Stir with ice until cold and blended.
Strain into cocktail glass. Garnish with orange peel.

JOAN RIVERS

This drink, based off a classic called the Stiletto, is named after a woman who (rumor has it) used to get stoned with Betty White back in the day. We can totally picture them drinking this weed-infused whiskey cocktail out of one of Joan's shoes.

- 1½ ounces weed-infused blended whiskey
- 1½ teaspoons Amaretto
- ½ ounce lemon juice
- Lemon peel garnish

Stir well with ice in old-fashioned glass.
Garnish with lemon peel.

WARD FOUR-TWENTY

This cannabis-laced version of a Ward Eight, a classic that extends back to before Prohibition, can also be served as a shooter without ice. Have a sip and wonder when marijuana's Prohibition will come to an end.

2 ounces weed-infused blended whiskey
½ ounce lemon juice
¼ ounce simple syrup
½ teaspoon grenadine
Lemon slice garnish

Shake with ice until cold and blended.
Strain into a highball glass over ice.
Garnish with lemon slice.

OUZO HAZE

If there's a drink with the word "Haze" in its name, we had to create a weed-infused version. Luckily, this drink also contains Ouzo, the Greek entry into the anise-flavored liqueur canon, which goes beautifully with the herby infusion.

1½ ounces weed-infused blended whiskey
2 teaspoons simple syrup
½ ounce lemon juice
1 teaspoon Ouzo
Flaming lemon peel garnish

Stir whiskey, simple syrup, and lemon juice with ice until old and blended. Float Ouzo on top. Bend lemon peel and squeeze over a lit match to ignite its oils. Garnish drink with flaming lemon peel.

NEW YORKER

The herbiness of weed-infused whiskey is brought out with the unique bittersweet flavor of grenadine in this take on the classic.

1½ ounces weed-infused Irish whiskey
½ ounce lime juice
¼ ounce simple syrup
¼ teaspoon grenadine
Lemon and orange peel garnish

Shake with ice until cold and blended.
Strain into cocktail glass.
Garnish with lemon and orange peels.

BROAD CITY

This complex cocktail with an unexpectedly goofy garnish was originally called the Ladies' Night, so naturally we had to call our weed-infused version the Broad City. Enjoy it with your best gal pal while watching *BC*, doing bong rips, and trading Bed, Bath, & Beyond coupons.

1¾ ounces weed-infused Irish whiskey
1 teaspoon anisette
2 dashes Angostura bitters
Pineapple wedge garnish

Stir well with ice and strain into cocktail glass.
Garnish with pineapple wedge and drink while wearing a dog hoodie.

LUCK OF THE HIGHRISH

The Irish are known more for their drinking than their love of the herb, but marijuana infuses beautifully into blended Irish whiskey. Crème de menthe and mint add even more fresh and herby flavor.

1½ ounces weed-infused Irish whiskey
½ ounce dry vermouth
1 teaspoon green crème de menthe
Mint sprig garnish

Stir with ice until cold and blended.
Strain into cocktail glass. Garnish with mint sprig.

FLAMING SPANISH

The flames in this tasty drink come when you burn its sugar-and-lime juice rim, causing a delicious burnt sugar taste that complements weed-infused whiskey nicely.

Burnt sugar and lime juice rim
1 dash triple sec
2 dashes overproof rum
1½ ounces coffee liqueur
1 ounce weed-infused blended whiskey
Coffee
Grated nutmeg garnish

Dip the rim of a martini glass in lime juice and then in sugar. Add the rum and Triple Sec. With a long match, carefully light the liquor while swirling the glass, melting the sugar on the rim. Pour in the coffee liqueur and whiskey, then top with coffee. Gently stir. Garnish with grated nutmeg.

MARY JANE'S MAI TAI

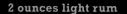

This classic cocktail pairs the citrus notes of weed with orange and lime for a drink that's fantastic in the summertime.

2 ounces light rum
1 ounce weed-infused dark rum
¾ ounce triple sec
½ ounce almond-orgeat syrup
¾ ounce lime juice
Lime wheel garnish

Shake with ice until cold and blended.
Strain into tiki glass over ice.
Garnish with lime wheel.

KINGSTON NEGRONI

Bob Marley would be proud of this downright Rastafarian Negroni. Make sure to use Jamaican rum to make it authentic!

   1 ounce weed-infused rum
   1 ounce sweet vermouth
   1 ounce Campari
   Orange peel garnish

Stir with ice until cold and blended.
Strain into double rocks glass with ice.
Garnish with orange peel.

MARIJUANA MILLIONAIRE

This classic cocktail was created during Prohibition, when people were drinking off the dregs of their liquor cabinets. Serve it today and people will have a hard time placing what liquors it contains, giving it a mysterious, speakeasy feel.

   ¾ ounce weed-infused dark rum
   ¾ ounce sloe gin
   ¾ ounce apricot brandy
   1 ounce lime juice
   Dash of grenadine
   Lime wheel garnish

Shake with ice until cold and blended.
Strain into cocktail glass and garnish with lime wheel.

RUMBO

While you may think of punches as "girly" drinks, they were actually invented by sailors who made use of locally available ingredients (craft cocktails!) to make giant batches of booze for their shipmates. They could have easily used their long journey to infuse a bottle of rum for this take on a classic.

- **7 ounces weed-infused dark rum**
- **1½ ounces banana liqueur**
- **3 ounces lime juice**
- **1½ ounces orange juice**
- **1½ ounces guava syrup**
- **Lime slices garnish**

In a series of shakers, shake with ice until cold and blended. Strain into a cooler with spout. Serve over rocks in cocktail glasses. Garnish with lime slices.

ROCKABILLY JUICE

This boozy iced tea was created by the Sailor Jerry rum company and only gets better with the addition of pot.

   2 ounces weed-infused dark or spiced rum
   2 ounces black iced tea
   ½ ounce lemon juice
   ½ ounce triple sec
   Lemon wedge garnish

Shake with ice until cold and blended.
Strain into a highball glass over ice.
Garnish with lemon wedge.

BEE'S NEST

This simple, warmed drink could be a cold cure, except that it tastes too delicious. Adding weed will catch even more bees than the honey.

   1½ ounces weed-infused dark rum
   ½ ounce honey syrup
   1 pat weed butter
   Boiling water

Add rum, honey syrup, and weed butter to a rocks glass.
Top up with boiling water. Stir until butter is dissolved
and well-mixed.

AMER

ADLE OF LIFE

. . . .

[...]g cocktail that tastes like an
[...]ai was created by the bar-
[...]e Dutch Kills bar in Queens
[...]ct for weed-infused rum.

[...]s weed-infused dark rum
[...]reen chartreuse
[...]emon juice
[...]ime juice
[...]range juice
[...]lmond-orgeat syrup
[...]ngostura bitters
[...] garnish

Shake rum, juice,
almond-orgeat syrup,
and bitters with ice
until cold and blended.
Strain into tiki glass over
ice. Pour green chartreuse
into hollowed-out lime half
and set on top of drink.
Light on fire. Let flames
burn out before serving.

GINGER SPICE

. . . .

We'll tell you what we want, what we really, really
want: this easy-to-drink rum and ginger ale drink
that was named before the Spice Girls were even
a thing.

1½ ounces weed-infused spiced rum
3 ounces ginger ale
Lime wedge garnish

Pour infused rum into highball glass over ice.
Top with ginger ale. Stir. Garnish with lime wedge.

OLD IRONSIDES

. . . .

Sip this dark and brooding contemporary classic on a cold winter's night while staring into its ruby-red depths and you're sure to have deep thoughts.

2 ounces weed-infused spiced rum
½ ounce Kirschwasser
½ ounce Cynar
Cherry garnish

Stir with ice until cold and blended.
Strain into a rocks glass with a large ice cube.
Garnish with cherry.

FIREPLACE BLAZE

. . . .

Cold outside? Throw some logs on the fire and get ready to get blazed with this hot and spicy cider.

2 ounces weed-infused dark rum
6 ounces hot apple cider
1 stick cinnamon
1 whole clove
1 dash orange bitters
Lemon wedge garnish

Pour into a mug. Let sit 3 minutes before serving.
Garnish with lemon wedge.

THE GREEN AND THE ORANGE

Add an extra touch of the green (the herbal kind) to this warm Irish nightcap that features whiskey and orange juice.

- 1½ ounces Irish whiskey
- ½ ounce orange juice
- ½ ounce lemon juice
- 4 ounces water
- 1 teaspoon sugar
- 2 dashes Angostura bitters
- 2 whole cloves
- 1 pat weed butter
- Grated nutmeg and lemon peel garnish

Add all ingredients except for the garnish to a microwave-safe glass. Heat in microwave in 10–15 second increments until butter is melted and drink is warm. Garnish with grated nutmeg and lemon peel.

RTY PUNCH

IN REDBEARD

queur
m—
f lime,
, and a
nd—
this
ur
d by
tender
ll.

- 10 ounces weed-infused dark rum
- 10 ounces pineapple juice
- 3¾ ounces lime juice
- 1¼ ounces velvet falernum
- 1¼ ounces grenadine
- 1¼ ounces simple syrup
- 10 dashes Angostura bitters
- Grated nutmeg and lime wheels garnish

kers, shake with ice until cold and blended. Strain into punch
ice cubes. Garnish with grated nutmeg and lime wheels.

BUTTERED BOURBON S

If you have weed butter
and no time for making
brownies, zap it in the
microwave and make this
quick shot that will have
you buzzing in no time.

2 ounces bourbon
1 pat weed butter, m
½ ounce simple syr

Stir bourbon and simple syrup in shot glass.
Pour weed butter on top and shoot!

HOT BUTTERED RUM

Probably one of the most common weed-infused
drinks thanks to the availability of weed butter,
you haven't really tried this winter classic until
you've had the chronic version.

2 whole cloves
2 whole allspice berries
1-inch stick cinnamon
1 teaspoon sugar (more to taste)
1½ ounces light rum, warmed
½ ounce dark Jamaican rum, warmed
Boiling water
1 pat weed butter

Place cloves, allspice, cinnamon, and sugar into a mug
with 2 bar-spoonfuls of boiling water. Let stand 5 minutes.
Then add warmed rums, 2 more ounces boiling water,
and weed butter. Stir until butter dissolves. Add more
sugar to taste.

NOT YOUR PTA'S PUMPKIN SPICE LATTÉ

Pumpkin spice turns rebel in this warm drink spiked with weed butter. Make sure to hide it from the kids!

2 ounces Irish cream
1 ounce vanilla vodka
1 pat weed butter, melted
3 ounces light cream
2 teaspoons brown sugar
¼ ounce cinnamon syrup
Grated nutmeg garnish

Add to a mug and warm in microwave in 10–15 minute increments until butter is dissolved and drink is warm. Stir until butter is fully incorporated. Garnish with grated nutmeg.

ORANGE BLUNT

You'll feel a bit like a mobster drinking this cocktail, which looks like coffee in a wine glass until you notice its devious underbelly. Substitute weed-infused cream for the weed butter if it's what you have on hand.

2½ ounces rum (preferably sugarcane-based)
1½ ounces light cream
1 pat weed butter, melted
2 dashes orange bitters
Coffee
Orange peel garnish

Shake rum, cream, weed butter, and bitters without ice until melted butter is incorporated. Pour into wine glass. Top with coffee. Garnish with orange peel. Serve with a cigar.

THE BIG LEBOWSKI

Infusing heavy cream with weed is a lot like making weed butter. This is one of only two recipes we have in this book using it, but for some dudes, it's the only recipe you need.

> 1½ ounces vodka
> 1½ ounces coffee liqueur
> 1 ounce weed-infused heavy cream

Pour into a rocks glass over ice. Stir.

FLAMER

GIRL SCOUT COOKIES

This ridiculously tasty dessert drink is served in a glass rimmed with Fluff and graham cracker crumbs, but that's just the sideshow to the flaming-marshmallow garnish. Make your weed-infused cream with a strain of Girl Scout Cookies for extra double entendre.

> 3 tablespoons graham cracker crumbs
> 2 tablespoons marshmallow Fluff
> 2 ounces caramel or vanilla vodka
> 2 ounces chocolate syrup
> 1 ounce weed-infused heavy cream
> 1 ounce overproof rum
> Flaming mini marshmallows garnish

Rim martini glass with graham cracker crumbs by dipping it Fluff, then cracker crumbs. Shake vodka, chocolate syrup, and weed-infused cream with ice until cold and blended. Strain into glass. String mini marshmallows on a skewer and lay over glass. Float overproof rum on top. Light it with a long lighter.

Serve when flame has burned out and marshmallows are toasted.

≥≪ INDEX ≫≤